BE THE SOUL MATE YOU
WANT TO ATTRACT

Be the Soul Mate You Want to Attract

STEP INTO YOUR SOVEREIGNTY AND MAGNETIZE A HIGHER LOVE

Jeanne Sullivan Billeci

The Soul Mate Coach

PRELIMINARY NOTES

Welcome! I'm looking forward to collaborating with you on your soul mate magnetizing journey! Below are a few important clarifications on terms I use in the book, as well as how to make the most of the worksheets.

Welcome Video: We're going to spend some intimate time together on this journey. I'll share some vulnerable things about my process, so you can truly understand that I have been in your shoes. I want to spare you some of the unnecessary pain I went through, and fast track your success. Sometimes it helps in the trust process to put a face to the name, so I put a welcome video on my website, *www.MySoulMateCoach.com* and my Facebook page, *@MySoulMateCoach*. You'll see a few references in the book to online resources available on these platforms, including meditations.

Worksheets: The worksheets in this book are intended for people who have invested in the book to fast track their soul mate magnetizing process. It's important that people using the worksheets read the book as they do the worksheets, to provide the needed context and explanation before and after completing them. They are designed to work in tandem with each other so that the reader can get the most out of them. This is a guided journey! Now that I've clarified that important point, I invite you to use these worksheets as many times as you need to. I have provided extra PDF versions of them on my website, *www.MySoulMateCoach.com* so you can fill them in online if you need to revisit them. They are also there if you need to print them out and do them by hand. Although it's important to stay as green as possible, it's sometimes helpful to unlocking information by freehand writing. If this is you, please honor that process without judging yourself. You can use recycled paper if you are conflicted about it.

Spirituality: For ease of reading, I will occasionally use the term "universe" and "higher power" interchangeably to express a spiritual power greater than ourselves, whatever that means to you. I don't want to exclude any spiritual belief systems with this book. The techniques in this book work whether you believe in God, Buddha, angels, spirit guides or any other higher power. If you don't believe in a higher power, you can think of it as your highest self, your intuition or your most enlightened self.

Sexual Pronouns: Also for ease of reading, I occasionally use traditional he/she pronouns in the book where necessary to the point I am making. This in no way is meant to disrespect anyone who prefers "they" or rejects traditional gender identity. I embrace the full spectrum and hope you will stay with me, as this book can help anyone who identifies with the "this book is for you" list on page 3.

Contents

Introduction

When I made my soul mate shift, I attracted my husband in 24 hours.

For real.

If it happened for me, it can happen for you.

I can't promise yours will arrive literally overnight, but he, she or they *will* come much faster if you take the steps I'm about to share—and give it everything you've got.

Contrary to popular belief, you *don't* have to heal everything either. That's where your soul mate comes in—but we'll get to that later.

THIS BOOK IS FOR YOU IF...

◆ You're tired of attracting the same relationship over and over—or no relationship at all—and want to get off the hamster wheel.

◆ You're approaching or are well into mid-life and you're afraid your dating pool is the size of a shot glass. You believe or fear that all the good ones are taken.

◆ You're worried you can't attract someone worthy who can bring something to your party and accept your authentic self.

◆ You're wary of losing yourself in a relationship again.

◆ You fear being vulnerable because you've made mistakes in the past and don't trust yourself.

◆ You think you're too fat, old or [fill-in-the-blank]

to attract the right partner (I was 44 and 300 pounds when I attracted my partner so let's put that to rest).

◆ You consider yourself spiritual and are open to concepts like law of attraction or a higher power aiding your transformation.

◆ You aren't sure you're good enough to attract the type of soul mate you really want.

◆ You feel defeated by the modern dating process and need a new approach that feels better.

◆ You've grown up enough emotionally to seek a mature relationship between two perfectly imperfect people rather than a fairytale romance.

HERE'S WHAT YOU'LL LEARN IN THIS BOOK

I've been where you are and know what to do. I spent tens of thousands of dollars learning from dating and relationship masters and will share my key learnings to save you precious time and money. I leveraged these insights with my experience as a certified law of attraction coach and relationship coach—and as a woman who has been with her soul mate for nearly 10 years—to help you recognize, attract and keep your soul mate relationship.

I include worksheets to collaborate with you on practical, tangible ways to do an efficient and compassionate overhaul on your mindset, so you can get your ideal life path and manifest a kindred soul mate relationship much faster. The process of living your best life does *not* need to take years and does *not* need to be complete before attracting your soul mate. You just need to be clear about what your best life looks like, release resistance to it, make some goals and take inspired action. This in turn will raise your vibration, which will attract people with a similar vibe.

How? Quantum physicists have proven that we are all fundamentally energetic beings, and research indicates that a being's energy projects out information to the world. I say the world because studies show that living cells can actually communicate over distance at the subatomic level. There's way more to be found if you follow this fascinating finding, but I bring it up because it explains to me why your energetic vibration projects a certain informational frequency out there, and other beings who recognize that frequency respond at the subatomic level—even if they are on the other side of the planet.

This was proven true for me years ago after I became a certified Reiki Master. During my training, we learned how to send reiki from a distance. I was traveling in California, and suddenly I felt an intense feeling that a friend in Miami was feeling despair. This is a friend I rarely saw and spoke to, and when I did it was always at the restaurant he owned. The feeling was so strong that I honored it and sent him reiki. Imagine my surprise when my phone rang during that moment and it was him. He had never called my cell before, so I didn't know it was him. When I heard his voice, I got chills. He said, "This is going to sound really weird, but I was really feeling down and didn't know what to do. I wished you were here to talk to and suddenly I felt your energy, like you were here in the room with me."

It's very common these days to say that we're all connected, and that has been my experience. That's why my goal with this book is to raise your energetic vibration—the information you are putting out in the world—so you can attract higher energetic soul mates than you have been. Our thoughts influence our emotions—all of which communicate a certain frequency that others will miss or see depending on their own frequency.

I hope you give the exercises in the book your best effort, as I believe they will shift your thinking and emotional patterns so you can put your best self out there.

With that being said, if your heart is cracked open just enough to allow a new perspective, and you're willing to move forward in baby steps or leaps, here's what you'll learn from this book:

◆ How to live your best life now so you can attract your ideal soul mate much faster.

◆ How to channel your inner superhero/diva/drag queen/leading lady or man to start living more courageously and authentically, which will compress the timeline between you and your ideal mate.

◆ Why you keep attracting the wrong kind of person and what to do about it.

◆ Bust the top relationship myths and transform limiting beliefs that keep you stuck.

◆ How to date more effectively so you don't feel depleted or get warts from kissing frogs.

◆ What a soul mate is and how to recognize them, so you don't keep missing them.

◆ Why you don't trust yourself and how to shift that.

◆ Why you need to stop waiting until you've healed everything to start on your quest.

◆ How to better market yourself so your soul mate finds you and recognizes you.

Some of the tips and insights shared in this book might be things you've heard before, but you weren't ready to process them or act upon them. That's okay. There are many wonderful dating and relationship gurus out there, but when the student is ready, the teacher they need at that moment appears to present the information in just the right way to reach them. It's important to be kind to yourself rather than beat yourself up with statements like "I knew that already—why didn't I act on it sooner?"

I gently invite you to let that kind of internal dialogue go as it doesn't serve you. You haven't wasted any time. Let me say that again—you have not wasted any time. Everything you have experienced up until now has made you clearer about what you do and don't want and can illuminate what your blocks are if you use a new lens. This book aims to be a set of new prescription glasses to help you see your patterns more clearly, so you can move past them and attract an ideal mate.

Every soul has its own divine timeline, and your soul needed to learn some things about itself in order to make the shift you are now ready to make. To compress the timeline between you and your soul mates, it requires a certain amount of self-love and a smidgeon of bravery to get back on the horse again. That means not just mounting the horse but nudging that horse ahead—walking or galloping—into the unknown while waving your freak flag. And don't worry; if one soul mate isn't ready, others will be.

You just need to shift so that you can reel in rather than repel what's best for you.

THE CLIFF'S NOTES ON THE 5 STEPS
TO ATTRACTING YOUR IDEAL MATE

You don't need to heal everything to get your soul mate here much faster. But you *do* have to shift, starting now, with these key 5 steps, which I'll expand on in this book. I've essentially created your informal Soul Mate Attraction Plan for you, so you can take action immediately, raise your vibration and manifest the love you want in much less time. My goal here isn't to provide immediate gratification, but to help you quickly remove your blocks to love, transform your attitude and raise your vibration so you can be the ideal soul mate you want to attract. Just by reading this book—and doing the exercises in these main 5 steps below—you will automatically become more magnetic to your mate, compressing the timeline between you and your soul mate(s) physically meeting.

1 FORGIVE yourself and others for what happened before and see everything as a lesson that got you prepared for a better path.

2 RELEASE RESISTANCE to love and clarify your ideal relationship, so you can get into alignment with manifesting the right love for you.

3 BE THE HERO/HEROINE of your own story, rewriting the old narrative of who you are and taking simple steps to being the soul mate you want to attract.

4 TRUST YOURSELF and the process, letting go of the expectation that history will repeat itself and shifting to more productive thinking so you can expect success with gratitude.

5 MARKET YOURSELF to show you believe in the product (you!).

The process for this shift is not linear, and that's perfectly fine. For example, you might find yourself on Step 4 and suddenly something in your environment triggers a negative memory, temporarily sending you back to the forgiveness work in Step 1. *Do not* worry if that happens to you. You can work on forgiveness for that issue and return to where you left off before this discovery. *However*, if something major does arise—such as a suppressed trauma—consider talking with a trusted therapist and pick up these exercises later. If you need a little extra help, your intuition will know.

MY STORY

Before I share all my secrets on how to magnetize your soul mate—starting now—I'm briefly going to share my backstory so that you can truly see I understand where you're coming from. It took a long time for me to even see my blocks, so it took all the longer to break through them. However, once I decided I really wanted my life to change for the better, and committed to it, everything shifted very quickly.

Although I soared high in my career at a young age, when it came to love I was late to the party. I struggled with obesity throughout my childhood, and in college I was told repeatedly that no one would ever want me. As I got older, I learned that some men were attracted to bigger girls, but I believed they didn't see me as a person.

When I decided to lose the weight in young adulthood, and got thin, I was frightened by all the sexual attention I was suddenly getting. I was also angry. I remember dreaming that I was floating above myself standing underneath a streetlamp in the rain. Random people were approaching me and saying or doing unkind things, and I looked up at my floating self and gave a primal scream.

That was the first time I really understood how enraged I was by how society treats you if you don't exactly fit in. Most of us can relate in some way to that. Maybe you didn't fit into our ultra-judgmental society's idea of the norm in some way. Maybe you were "too fat" or "too skinny," your nose or ears were "too big," or you laughed "too loud," or you dressed "weird" or you were "too geeky" or "too plain." Or maybe you were targeted for being gay, transgender, or entertaining people in drag. Maybe you were called "selfish" because you didn't want children or were labeled an "old maid" or "serial dater" because you didn't marry before 35.

The list goes on and on.

We are often criticized for being different, and we leap to the obvious conclusion that we must hide our authentic selves so that potential mates will like us. The opposite is true, but we are taught to hide so we don't bore someone or scare them away. We'll talk more about this later, but for now just know that this is the main reason dating often sucks so much and is so draining of our heart energy. Keeping up this charade is exhausting and simply doesn't work in the long run. It is only by being your authentic self—seen with a loving filter—that makes you truly magnetic to your true tribe. There is nothing more beautiful than being surrounded by people who adore the real you—warts included!

BACK TO YOU

Okay now that you have the Cliff's Notes on how to become more magnetic to your soul mate(s), it's time to get back to you! If you haven't met one of your soul mates—and I believe there are many out there whom you could be happy with—and you've been looking a while, you might be discouraged. Especially these days of the #MeToo movement, which has stirred up a lot of anger and fear.

Perhaps you're like me and have done a lot of seminars, therapy and even psychic readings trying to figure out why it hasn't yet happened for you. Maybe after you tried everything and eliminated all potential causes for not finding them in *this* life, you've resorted to exploring what was blocking you from your *past* lives. I'm not ashamed to say I did that too!

The good news is, as a certified coach who has traveled this journey, I learned a *lot* along the way about why some people haven't yet manifested their soul partner. I've shared those key learnings with coaching clients and friends who were frustrated in their own soul mate search. They've encouraged me to write a book, so here we are. My intention is to help people like you un-cover and break through your blocks, so you can become more magnetic and compress the timeline between you and your soul mate. The world needs more soul mate partners now more than ever, and I don't want you to spend 25 years looking for yours like I did.

I'm excited for you! By taking this step, your soul is telling me you are ready to make the shift to your highest expression, and you are willing to act. I believe you were led to this book because this approach is energetically right for you. You can and will attract an ideal mate! Of course, divine timing plays a role in when you meet, but I firmly believe that your inner transfor-mation can greatly accelerate the process. I've coached many people through the process of manifesting their desires, once they're ready to grow and receive their greater good. When you attract this partner, you'll soon discover you haven't reached a destination. It's just the beginning of a new journey of continued transformation.

Although we will touch on serious themes, I invite you to take on an attitude of curiosity, playfulness and humor—and trust in the process—as we explore how to make your Soul Mate shift—and what to do *after* you make it so you enjoy the ride. Buckle your seat belt and let's get going on this spiritual road trip to your soul mate!

DECIDE TO GET OFF THE HAMSTER WHEEL

Sometimes when we're dating—or contemplating it—we get a bit discouraged by what can seem like a never-ending pattern of attracting dead-end relationships. This is what I call the hamster wheel. You are expending a lot of energy—both physical, mental and spiritual—without moving forward.

We see this and yet we don't know what else to do, so we keep doing it, hoping our luck will change and produce better results. We tell ourselves it's just not the right time and we just give up, letting ourselves off the hook.

Please don't do that. While there is some divine timing involved in the timing of your ideal mate's arrival, you *do* have a say in how quickly you become ready. Your readiness will automatically make you more magnetic.

I believe you bought this book because a higher part of you knows it's time to get off the hamster wheel and get what you want. That highest expression of you knows you can absolutely attract your ideal mate and do powerful things in the world together—and that you deserve it. But if you've been at this a while and feel discouraged, the part of you in pain is resisting it. Maybe not consciously resisting it—but blocked all the same.

I was on that wheel 10 years ago. I not only got off the wheel, but my life now is unrecognizable in the best way. Step by step, I learned how to be the soul mate I wanted to attract and magnetized him. We helped each other grow and now we are in careers that are aligned with our true purpose. Perhaps we both would have gotten there on our own eventually, but I know our partnership brought it faster. Why? The experience of being in a relationship serves as a mirror to help us see where we need to grow and what we want to change. Soul mate relationships push our buttons like no other and inspire us to evolve all the faster.

I want that for you, and I know you can have it.

ARE YOU READY TO MOVE FORWARD?

Before we jump in, I invite you to go within and ask yourself:

◆ "Am I willing to do what it takes to get off the hamster wheel and make space for a soul mate?"

◆ "Am I willing to try a new approach that might feel a little awkward at first to be the soul mate I really want?"

◆ "Am I willing, once my soul mate arrives, to allow them in and make the effort to create and sustain a healthy relationship?"

If the answer is yes to these, but you feel a little nervous or unsure, that's okay. All you need right now is the willingness.

If the answer is "I'm not sure" to any of these, but you still want to move forward, that's okay too. Here are some reasons why you may be feeling this way, and why I hope you proceed anyway.

It might mean that you need the exercises in this book to gain some clarity.

It could be that you feel resentment because you perceive that attracting a soul mate has come so easily for others and it's really hard for you.

Or it might mean there's a major trauma that needs addressing with therapy.

Feeling these emotions doesn't mean you can't move forward, but it may mean the process could take a little longer for you. These feelings are simply resistance and give clues to a mindset that is keeping you from flowing into the future that is meant for you. If you are conscious of these emotions, it's actually a good thing because awareness of thoughts that are holding you back is key to shifting.

It's all about *making the decision* to move out of "Groundhog Day" mode and move forward, even if they are baby steps. Any momentum is a win!

EXERCISE 1: THE COST OF NOT MOVING FORWARD
To help motivate you, go ahead and get comfortable and close your eyes. Imagine yourself a year from now, in the exact same metaphoric place in your life that you are now. Allow yourself to feel whatever comes up for you.

How was that for you?

If it felt good, great! That can mean you are living your best life and if a soul mate happens to arrive, it will just enhance an already great gig. It can also mean you are not quite sure you want a soul mate in your life, because you fear they might mess up a good thing. If this is you, it's a good idea to get quiet and meditate on how you would feel to have someone in your space much of the time, bringing moments of joy but also requiring your energy and effort. If there are feelings of worry or doubt, explore what it is you are afraid of. As Abraham-Hicks said in the book "Ask and It Is Given" your feelings are the ultimate guide to whether you're in alignment with your true path. If you feel this conflict, but a deeper part of you wants to proceed, you are in the *right* place. This book is designed to help release any resistance you have and become more magnetic to someone who can bring something to your party!

It's important to mention I've known some fabulously successful and happy people who did not want a soul mate. They wouldn't have picked up this book, but if you know someone like this, trust me when I say that when you experience the joy of being with your mate, you may be tempted to try and get your single friends coupled up. It's wonderful to want to share the happiness you are feeling, but it's important to respect that everyone is on their own journey and knows what is best for them. If they do decide they want a soul mate, your radiance will prompt them to ask you how you were able to attract the right person.

Okay, now. If imagining yourself a year from now felt negative—frustrating, sad, frightening or just wrong somehow—then you are also in the right place. This book is designed to help free yourself from your patterns and get on the ideal path for you!

Let me reassure you that if you really, really want a soul mate, and you release resistance to the entire experience of it—the good, the bad and the occasional ugly that comes with it, and become crystal clear on what you want—that person or people will come. If you think I am throwing shade at you by implying that this mate hasn't arrived because of you, I am absolutely not. It is you, but not because there is anything wrong with you. I know that each one of you reading these words is beautiful and spectacular in your own unique way. Every soul is born pristine, connected and magnetic. Just look at how attractive any baby is—because they haven't learned to question their value. Over time, their dark experiences can teach them to question their divinity and the abundance they deserve. Even if your life is great overall, but you just haven't manifested the right person to share it with, it just means you need to be a detective and find out where the resistance is.

Are you ready to find out? Let's do it!

Imagine yourself a year from now and your soul mate is with you. Don't try to picture what they look like. Just feel their presence or see their soul in light form. Tap into how you feel with that person with you—not rescuing you, but rather, supporting you. Allow yourself to imagine what you'd be doing with that person, or without them knowing they are there supporting you. When you get to that place, enjoy it for as long as you can and then come back here.

How was that? On a scale of 1 to 10, how much do you want that life?

If you feel like it's a 7 or higher, use that intensity to remind yourself throughout this journey why you are doing this. In anything that takes effort, there must be a higher vision propelling you, making it worth it. If your score was lower, you might not feel motivated enough yet to take this journey, and that's okay. Trust yourself and what your spirit is telling you.

If you feel ready to continue, let's do it!

EXERCISE 2: VISUALIZE WHAT IT WILL BE LIKE OFF THE HAMSTER WHEEL

Let's celebrate your first step off the hamster wheel and on to your ideal life path with a powerful ritual. I like to do this ritual on New Year's Eve—a time when many people think of ringing out the old and ringing in the new. If you think about it, today is New Year's for your spirit, so let's set the stage for partying!

1. Set the Mood

Find a space you love and get out a pen and paper. If you have a nice notebook or journal that would feel more pleasurable, go ahead and get it. It's important that you use your hand to write on a piece of paper rather than a computer. Technology has a way of keeping us in our heads, and this exercise is all about reconnecting to the heart and spirit. Your body and its sensations are the clearest interpreters of your intuition, so let's keep it old school.

The space should be somewhere you can feel good and nurtured. It could be a corner of your house where you have a pretty view or an altar. If so, you could enhance your pleasure with any props that help you feel expansive, from candles and incense to inspiring music. If your spirit would feel more inspired in nature, grab your writing materials and head to the beach, forest, desert or whatever you can access.

2. Meditate/Imagine

Even if you've never meditated, you can do this simple exercise. I did it with a dear friend who had some control issues and always said he couldn't meditate. I gave him permission to suck at it. This exercise doesn't require perfect meditation skills. It just requires a quiet space to let your imagination run free and to focus. In fact, if the word meditate intimidates you, just look at it as an imagining. When he was free of the self-judgmental expectation of doing it perfectly, he had a very powerful visualization.

Make sure you are sitting up with your feet planted on the floor or ground. Lying down could make you fall asleep, and you need to be conscious for this one. Now, if you need a voice to guide you along this process, you can ask a trusted loved one to help, or you can record your own voice and play it back, so you don't have to try and memorize this. I also of-fer a "Get Off the Hamster Wheel Meditation" on my website, *www.MySoulMateCoach.com* under the meditations page.

Take a few slow, deep breaths. As you breathe in, imagine yourself allowing in a loving, beautiful, healing light from a higher power—Mother Earth, the Universe, God, an angel, a power animal, a spirit guide, or even your own soul—the part of you that is fully connected to source, love and wisdom. As you breathe out, imagine yourself releasing any negative energy—self-doubt, anger, frustration, hurt, fear—to your higher power, who takes it away and transmutes it so it can no longer harm you.

Imagine your higher power sending you this healing, loving light into your feet, soothing, relaxing, comforting you, filling any empty spaces left from the released negative energy. Allow this light to travel up in stages to your legs, hips, stomach, chest and throat. When it gets to your forehead, which is the seat of your intuition, see the light opening that channel so more infor-mation can come in. See the light going up through the top of your head, connecting you to your higher power, who reflects the light back at you and amplifies it tenfold, surrounding you in a protective, healing and loving cocoon. This is the cocoon you will return to throughout the book---the chrysalis that you will soon shed and emerge a butterfly.

Imagine your "hamster wheel" or whatever form of cage you metaphorically see yourself in. Really see the cage and tap into the way it makes you feel. Notice its color, shape, texture and how it keeps you from that future you want. Peer through the cage and allow yourself to imagine the future that is being kept from you. See your future self as if you were an Olympic gold medalist on a pedestal, thrilled to have achieved your dreams. See your soul mate beside you—the one who supported your journey here. Imagine the joy and sense of accomplishment you feel. As you allow these feelings to amplify, see the cage that is keeping you from this future. Feel the frustration and sadness that stands in the way.

Now ask yourself, what are the patterns in my life that I want to break free of? What are the things that happen over and over that make me feel these negative emotions? These could be putting yourself down, putting others before yourself so much that you lose yourself, attracting relationships that can't provide what you want. Whatever these patterns are, allow yourself to see the ones that come up in this moment and acknowledge them, knowing that more may come to your consciousness throughout the exercises in the book.

Ask yourself, do I want to let these patterns go? Am I willing to let these patterns go?

If the answer is no, ask your higher power what keeps you from being willing? Is there trauma that is still highly charged within you and needs healing with therapy? If so, you may want to seek a therapist or self-help book to release this. Or is the resistance more about being more comfortable with the devil you know rather than an uncertain future? If that is the case, think back to a time when you took action to improve your situation and the result was better than you thought. Remind yourself that taking action can have positive results and imagine again how you'd feel to be in this prison a year from now.

Once you are willing, say to yourself, "I am ready and willing to break free. I am ready to take that first step right now towards the future I desire. I have decided it's time to be the soul mate I really, really want to attract."

See yourself stepping off the hamster wheel. Or see yourself opening the lock on your cage, opening the door and stepping through. Or maybe for you, it feels more empowering to bend the bars open with that super-human strength within you. With the support of your higher power, take another step towards that future vision. See the soul of your ideal mate waiting there, beckoning you. Take enough steps that you can turn around and look at the prison you just stepped away from.

Take a big deep breath and release it. Feel the relief and gratitude that you took this first step. Feel the joy that you no longer have to be in that place. Know that the only person who can put you back there is yourself. Say goodbye to that self-imposed prison and thank it for the lessons it taught you about who you are and what you want. Feel the gratitude for the pain that propelled you onto this beautiful new path.

Now turn back to your future and see the pedestal gently surrounded by a green flame, knowing that green is the color of manifestation. Knowing that you are a powerful creator of your reality, send energy from your heart to gently fuel and intensify the flame.

Say to yourself, "I am a powerful creator. I am excited to know that I am in the process of manifesting this future. I don't need to know how I will get there. I just need to keep my focus on my vision, releasing any resistance along the way and moving forward."

Say to your soul mate, "I am ready and willing to do whatever it takes to bring you into my life. Get ready for me—I am on my way." Feel the joy of your soul mate or imagine the light of their soul sparking in acknowledgment. Sit with all the feelings—especially gratitude—that this union brings, for at least two minutes.

When you are ready, allow the prison and the future to gently dissolve until you see only the cocoon. Acknowledge that you are always protected by this cocoon and can return to it whenever you need to get back into alignment. When you are ready, slowly come back to the room and gently open your eyes.

3. Celebrate!

Congratulations! In this moment you have already begun making the energetic shift that will compress the timeline between you and your soul mate. Take the time today to acknowledge this accomplishment. It's a very important part of the process to focus more on our accomplishments rather than the failures of the past. They were just lessons.

How would you like to commemorate this moment? What would make you feel good? Would you like to get a spa treatment? Take a walk in nature? Watch your favorite movie? Dance in your living room? Take a bath with wine and candles? Whatever it is, I encourage you to do this alone, because sometimes even loved ones can unconsciously project their fears and doubts onto us when we take a step forward, and this moment of victory is yours to savor. Or perhaps you'd like to write down what no longer serves you and burn the paper in a ceremonial bowl, locking in the intention that you are releasing these patterns in this new year.

Whatever it is, do it before you go to bed while everything is fresh.

When you wake up, feel free to celebrate your spiritual New Year with something you really enjoy doing and don't normally take the time for.

Enjoy the holiday! Rather than rush the process, luxuriate in this moment and pat yourself on the back for getting started. If you feel like you want to sit with this vibration today, you can certainly pick this book back up tomorrow.

Are you ready to start magnetizing now?

PART ONE

"The weak can never forgive.
Forgiveness is the attribute
of the strong."

Mahatma Gandhi

T o continue the process of being your lovingly authentic self, I will offer some assignments to help release the reasons you believe deep down you are unlovable, undesirable or not worthy of your ideal partner. These are inaccurate beliefs that block you from allowing in your soul mate(s) and also your greatest good.

A key step in the process is the "F" word—Forgiveness. This means forgiving those—including yourself—who have caused you pain and created a wall to intimacy. When people hurt us, we tend to believe we deserved it, which is not true. Forgiveness is not about forgetting, but rather releasing the emotional attachment to the hurt and the belief behind it so we can move forward. In other words, forgiveness is an exercise of self-compassion and self-love.

First, let's dive into what forgiveness is and isn't.

FORGIVENESS IS...

◆ Conscious decision to let go of resentment or vengeance toward a person who has harmed you, regardless of whether they deserve forgiveness.

◆ An empowering process that brings the forgiver peace of mind and enables them to recognize their pain without letting it define them—so they can heal and move on.

WHAT FORGIVENESS ISN'T...

◆ Reconciliation with the person who hurt you.

◆ Pretending what hurt you didn't happen.

- Allowing the person to repeat the behavior over and over.

- Having no consequence for abusive behavior.

- Having the pain dissolve right away.

FORGIVENESS BENEFITS YOU, NOT THE PERPETRATOR

Forgiveness is for YOU. When we cannot forgive someone who hurt us, we remain attached to the hurt and cannot be free of that experience. This hurts you more than the "perpetrator" and you will likely continue to attract similar people and situations until you learn how to forgive. When you release the feeling that someone owes you something, you are freeing yourself from that baggage.

You're not excusing or denying the behavior that hurt you; you are releasing the attachment so you can empower yourself to move on, regardless of whether the person who harmed you—intentionally or unintentionally—feels remorse. Feeling attached to whether they feel remorse can be a prison, and you never want to give anyone that kind of power over your peace. From a spiritual perspective, it can be a big step towards enlightenment—if that is something you seek—to try and understand why the person was the way they were and forgive them for hurting you, as they didn't know any better.

We all hurt people—sometimes on purpose and sometimes unknowingly—but if you can see it as a lesson or reason to evolve rather as something that "broke" you—it will set you free. It doesn't mean you have any contact with this person. Sometimes people are not ready to evolve and take responsibility for their actions, and if contact keeps you from growing, or puts you in danger, forgiveness is just a tool to release the energetic cord between you and move on. And on a spiritual level, releasing that cord could be the action that soul needs to get unstuck.

One of the steps in an exercise coming up is to forgive yourself for any part you might have played in a situation that hurt you. I am not talking about sexual or physical abuse. This is about forgiving ourselves for any mistakes we played in situations where we got hurt.

For example, I was hurt for years when my former partner couldn't say I love you. He admitted at the end that he was selfish for holding on to the relationship when he couldn't offer what I needed. He had told me repeatedly he'd eventually be able to offer it, but finally realized he couldn't. For a long time, I was upset by the "wasted time" and the "lie." But really, I needed to forgive myself first for staying in the relationship for way longer than was healthy for me. I had to forgive myself for ignoring the inner voice that told me to leave but I ignored it because I was so desperate to find love and validation outside of myself. I had ignored and made excuses for his behavior—which showed clearly that he was a commitment phobic person—for very long.

With the help of a therapist, I owned my role in this drama with a man who couldn't properly love anyone until he healed his wounds.

Forgive myself I did, and I forgave him so I could move on. I didn't continue the friendship though, as he was not in therapy addressing his issues. The therapist warned me that until he got help, he would consciously or unconsciously sabotage any relationship I had under the guise of being a friend. He wouldn't want to be there as my partner, but part of him didn't want me with someone else.

It was challenging because people who liked him accused me of being petty for cutting him out of my life. But cutting him out, as hard as it was, was the greatest gift of self-love I could give myself. After a couple of weeks of tears--and processing old grief that was triggered by the loss—I started to dance and laugh again, which startled me. I realized how happy my soul was that I was no longer accepting so little, and could now in fact, move towards the happiness I deserved.

Another example might be that you hurt someone—maybe you were an addict and stole from a boyfriend or girlfriend to get money for drugs, or maybe you cheated on them. If you don't forgive yourself, there's a good chance you will sabotage future relationships as a way of punishing yourself.

FORGIVE AND MAKE SPACE FOR A HIGHER LOVE
Forgiveness is the key to breaking negative patterns and understanding you are worthy of better, so you can attract a higher love. To help you continue becoming more magnetic to that higher love, the next assignments focus on why you are worthy of love so you can start raising your vibration and attracting more positive experiences.

FORGIVENESS EXERCISES
As you do the exercises in this book, it's REALLY important to take a break in between each one, so you can process and integrate them. This is key to shifting your attitude and raising your vibration so that you can invite a higher love into your life—a

more evolved soul mate who will feel supported and want to stay.

I encourage each break to be marked by some form of self-care, such as a walk in nature, a meditation, a scented bath, a date with yourself—anything that makes you feel good. The goal is to lock in—or reinforce—the learning with acts of self-love, so you evolve organically and feel fully worthy of this higher love you desire. If you already feel worthy, great! These acts will feel natural for you. If you need a little help in that area, I've got your back. These are part of the homework and VERY necessary to the process. Please do them!

EXERCISE 1A: FORGIVING YOURSELF

Please do Exercise 1A on the next page. Here you will develop and meditate upon a Self-Forgiveness Statement.

Forgiving yourself is an important first step in breaking free from the blame and judgment you have heaped upon yourself. Even if a part of you feels you don't deserve forgiveness, please do this exercise anyway because I—and anyone who knows and loves you—know you deserve it. This exercise will help you shift out of any shame you feel and move on. You may feel like you need to do this a few times before it takes, and that's okay. We're not in a race here. You also may find yourself needing to forgive yourself in the future, and if so, you can use this exercise to remind yourself we all make mistakes and deserve forgiveness if we're willing to take responsibility.

If it's challenging to forgive yourself, and the memories bring back an ongoing cycle of shame, ask yourself if there is anything you can do to make amends with this person—without harming

EXERCISE 1A: FORGIVING YOURSELF

Take a moment to reflect on your actions in the past that you may regret. Ask yourself and journal the answers free-flow style—without editing:

- ◆ How has my refusal to forgive others harmed me? Is holding on to this resentment more painful than the incident?
- ◆ What mistakes did I make that I continue to feel guilty about?
- ◆ How am I punishing myself?
- ◆ Did I consciously or unconsciously blame and punish others for my mistake, and did that keep me stuck or harm others?
- ◆ What have I learned from my mistake? What positive things have come from it?
- ◆ How will forgiving myself improve my life?
- ◆ Do I deserve forgiveness? How do I positively impact others?

Once you reflect on these questions, fill in the blanks to create a –

Self-Forgiveness Statement

I forgive myself for ....

From this mistake I learned ....

....

and became a better person because ....

....

I make the world a better place by ....

....

I choose to let go of the past and allow in the greater good I deserve.

them further. Often, expressing an apology in any form will help you release yourself. If seeing you would harm the person emotionally, you can write a letter apologizing and share it with a therapist.

You could also try to release it in a burning bowl ceremony. This is a transformative ritual you might have heard friends doing on New Year's Eve. They typically write down any negative thoughts, pain or negative patterns that no longer serve them. They throw the paper into a fire-safe vessel, such as a fire pit, to symbolically release the negativity so they can ring in the new year with a clean slate. You can do this any time of year for yourself!

If you believe that apologizing wouldn't harm the person, it's important not to attach yourself to the outcome. This person doesn't owe you forgiveness, and that's okay. You release yourself by owning up to it and letting go of the shame. Whatever the lesson for them is, it's not for you to figure out, so if you have done what you can, it's time to let it go. Once you learn the lesson you can release the guilt and regret, and endeavor to treat others better moving forward. Remember that mistakes don't define us as "bad" but rather, they help us to grow.

If you have moments where the guilt returns, take out your Self-Forgiveness Statement and read it, focusing on the positive impact you have now and will in the future. Focus back onto the greater good you deserve.

Please take a break with an act of self-love so you can reflect on this exercise until it feels complete.

EXERCISE 1B: FORGIVING OTHER PEOPLE

Once you have forgiven yourself, the next step is to forgive those who have hurt you. Holding on to this resentment only keeps you attached energetically to this person—like a toxic cord. If you want to move forward and be free of these people, it's important to cut this cord lovingly by forgiving them.

Forgiving others does NOT mean you excuse anything they did that hurt you, but rather to acknowledge that everyone is in different places in their evolutionary journey and makes mistakes. Rather than hold on to that pain and stay stuck, forgiveness is purely for you to move on.

Are you ready to set yourself free? **Do Exercise 1B on the facing page.** Please fill out this chart freely, without editing or self-judgment. First you will list the names of the people you need to forgive and how each of them harmed you—from your point of view.

Then you will go back and note any role you might have played in getting hurt. This means owning anything you did to contribute to the situation, from being overly sensitive and not setting healthy boundaries for yourself or respecting others' healthy boundaries. Perhaps you always thought of yourself as the victim in that situation, but upon a brave second look you realize that the other person was the victim, and you projected blame instead of taking responsibility. As many people do in 12-Step work, you gently, without self-judgment, ask if any of these resentments arise in part from your own fear, selfishness, inconsideration or dishonesty. If that is the case, just notice it gently and write it down. You may need to do Exercise 1A again if this comes up for you.

The Soul Mate Coach

EXERCISE 1B: FORGIVING OTHER PEOPLE

People I Need to Forgive	How did they hurt me?	What role did I play in getting hurt?**	What did I learn from this situation?	How will releasing this improve my life? Am I ready to let go?

** If this person sexually or physically abused you, do not ask yourself what role you played. No one asks for or deserves abuse. If this is something that applies to you, and you haven't sought therapy, please consider healing that trauma with a trained counselor.

If you're resisting this exercise a bit, gently remind yourself that forgiveness isn't about excusing but releasing attachment to that person through anger. The more you hold on to that grudge, it doesn't hurt them as much as you because you're the one stuck. Forgiving them and yourself is really for YOU.

After you have taken your self-love break, please read on!

EXERCISE 1C: FORGIVENESS STATEMENT
Please do Exercise 1C on the facing page, so you can break free of the hold that past hurts have upon you. Rather than excuse any bad behavior, this exercise is designed to help you release the attachment you have to the hurt, so you can get unstuck. This is really important because many of us stay stuck because there is a payoff to staying in the same place—whether it be feeling safe or not taking any appropriate responsibility for what happened.

Reflect on your finished statement when it feels complete and connect to the feeling of gratitude for how this situation has or will improve your life. Feel the gratitude for how this will help result in a healthier soul mate relationship and feel the joy as if this ideal relationship was already a part of your physical reality.

If reflecting upon and using the Forgiveness Statement isn't enough to move on, think about what you need in order to do so. If you have never addressed your grievance with this person, speak to them about it. It's important to get into a state of calm and curiosity, as radiating hurt or blame may make the other person defensive or retreat. By coming from a more balanced place, you are much more likely to learn the truth and find the healing. Use the "when you did this, I felt" structure so you are only talking about the behavior and owning your reaction to

EXERCISE 1C: FORGIVENESS STATEMENT

Use the insights in the Exercise 1B chart to create a Forgiveness Statement for people you are ready to forgive.

I forgive .... for ....

....

I forgive myself for my role, which was ....

....

....

I learned from this experience that ....

....

....

I will use this lesson to make mine and others' lives better by ....

....

....

I let go of my resentment and fear and focus instead on gratitude for the lesson and the positive benefits it will have on my future relation-ships.

the behavior. You may find it was a misunderstanding, or the person had no idea they hurt you, or they knew they did but were too embarrassed to speak to you. It's possible this person may apologize, and if you find that you played a role in the misunderstanding, own it gently by apologizing. It's important not to attach to the outcome. Express yourself for your own release, whether or not that person is ready to apologize or forgive. By taking responsibility, you have done what you can to rectify it, and now you can move on. They may learn their lesson later, but that is part of their journey. You may have planted a seed, and now it's up to them.

If the person you need to confront abused you, it's important you first talk with a professional therapist about it to make sure this is a healthy and safe decision for you.

Forgiveness is about taking your power back. A life well lived is your best revenge, so read your forgiveness statements when old resentments arise, and put your power and focus back on what you desire—a healthy soul mate relationship.

Please take a self-care break before moving on to the next exercise.

EXERCISE 1D: DO THE HO'OPONOPONO PRAYER
This ancient Hawaiian prayer can be a great way to forgive without confronting a person, and it's easy to do whenever you need to. Ho'oponopono means "to make right," and when you hold on to resentment, you can't be free because you are energetically connected to the person whom you believe wronged you. This prayer allows you to cut the cord and release the old narrative so you can create new and healthier existing relationships.

EXERCISE 1D: THE HO'OPONOPONO PRAYER

Start with self-forgiveness. When you are in a quiet place, relax into a meditative state by focusing on your breath. Then...

- ◆ Step 1: Tune in to the resentment that is keeping you stuck and say, "I'M SORRY."
- ◆ Step 2: Ask for forgiveness for the harm you caused yourself by holding on to anger and say "PLEASE FORGIVE ME."
- ◆ Step 3: Thank your higher self for its forgiveness and grace by saying, "THANK YOU."
- ◆ Step 4: Tune in to your enlightened self and the love it has for you, and say, "I LOVE YOU."

Say, "I'm sorry, please forgive me, thank you and I love you" as many times as you need to until it feels complete.

Then you can repeat this process for forgiving others at the soul level rather than the personality level. You're not excusing behavior or blaming anyone.

When you say, "I'm sorry," and "Please forgive me," you are taking responsibility for any part you might have unconsciously or consciously played in the rift or misunderstanding.

You also are owning the resentment you harbored which might have harmed the other person and releasing any guilt you might feel.

Then you say thank you for the forgiveness and send your unconditional love to the other soul that is still learning and evolving.

You can keep doing this prayer for every person you feel you need to forgive. What's interesting to me about this prayer is that you are apologizing to yourself and asking for your own forgiveness, even if you are ultimately trying to forgive someone else. To me this means you are taking responsibility for releasing yourself from resentment—or seeing yourself as a victim—so you can heal and move on.

There are many videos, books and websites devoted to this process if you'd like to explore it further.

EXERCISE 1E: SCHEDULE ACTS OF
SELF-KINDNESS INTO YOUR ROUTINE

Now that you've done this important work, give yourself time to integrate the learnings and honor your discoveries by practicing some self-kindness more regularly. Many people find it easier to be kind to others but skimp on themselves. Very often, especially with sensitive and giving people, it is in our nature to take care of others before ourselves, and self-care is the first sacrifice when we are short on time.

I've invited you to start making space for this through your breaks between exercises, but now it's time to make this a habit practiced every single day.

I hope you are proud of yourself for taking this step forward, and it's important you acknowledge it and treat yourself with the love and compassion you deserve. No one is perfect, and personal growth takes honesty and bravery. Lessons make us stronger and enable us to shift patterns that no longer serve us. Here are some ways you can nourish yourself:

◆ Small Acts of Kindness – Take a long bath, get a

massage, walk in nature, read a book or go to the gym.

◆ Recognize that mistakes don't define you; they make you better if you learn from them.

◆ Refocus on what you want, create a vision board, make a plan, etc.

◆ Clear up the clutter in your home so your space feels like a place you want to be and invite someone into.

◆ Seek support by talking to a coach, therapist or trusted friend.

◆ Go out and have fun, throw a party, create art or go to a movie.

◆ Do a loving kindness meditation.

Perhaps you have other ideas? If so, feel free to share them on Facebook *@MySoulMateCoach* with others who are sharing this journey with you. Whatever feels nurturing and supportive to you, please do it, starting now. It's an important part of processing and elevating your vibration, making you that much closer to your ideal relationship with yourself—which will make you more magnetic to that higher love you desire with a partner.

I invite you to take out your calendar—or use the worksheet on the following page—and start filling it with at least one of your favorite acts of self-kindness *every day*. Please spend enough time on these acts of self-kindness so that they feel nourishing rather than rushed. If you feel like doing more than one per day – good for you! Go for it!

EXERCISE 1E: SCHEDULING ACTS OF SELF-KINDNESS

MONTH

MON	TUES	WED	THURS	FRI	SAT	SUN

This is just a tool to get you in the habit of making space for self-nurturing, as people with full tanks tend to vibrate at a higher level and feel more deserving of receiving love rather than only giving. I invite you to do this every month until it feels like second nature. If you say to yourself, "I don't have time for this today," just gently notice that you are resisting your highest good. Go within and identify why and release it. If you procrastinated on doing this act of kindness for yourself and it's the end of the day, choose a quicker act and do it before you go to sleep. If doing your act means you have to say "no" or not "now" then please honor that boundary. It's really, really important that you don't allow yourself to skip these acts of kindness. We don't want them to be a chore you must scratch off the list, but rather something you look forward to.

If you truly just forget, gently forgive yourself and resolve to start again the next day. Now, please take a self-nourishing break, and when are ready, go ahead and move on to the next section.

Release

Resistance

"You're always one decision away
from a totally different life."

Mark Batterson

"You've gotta find a way to get out
of your own way, so you
can progress in life."

Steve Carlton

e will spend some time exploring ways we can re-connect with our intuition, which knows what is blocking us—but we are listening to others rather than our inner voice.

By others I mean people in your life who project their negative beliefs onto you, as well as the more insidious "other," which is lurking within you. Your inner "demons." A big part of my shift was facing my negative inner voice, who loved to tell me how I don't measure up or how true love was not in the cards for me. As I started contradicting that monstrous voice and got more empowered, I noticed big improvements in dating and relationships.

Speaking of monsters, let's start banishing yours, shall we? Or at least sending them to the backseat so your most empowered self can drive. While negative forces are a part of our duality of dark and light, it's important not to let them define us. In 12-step groups, addicts often share how they feared letting go of their addiction because they don't know what else was there. They didn't know who they were without it. That's an extreme example, but regardless what negative force you are struggling with, it's important to make sure the light inside of us—the highest expression of ourselves—is in charge so we can be happy, productive and help make the world a better place. In charge most of the time at least! I am grateful for my struggles because they motivated me to reach for a more inspired place.

Ready to start reaching for a more inspired place? Set aside some uninterrupted time so you can get the most of it and make the space as comfortable and pleasurable as you can. Maybe you want to add a little music or candles, and sink into a beanbag, diva throne chair, recliner or yoga mat. Maybe you'd like to pair the experience with a cozy cup of tea, coffee or scotch (I don't judge). I just invite you to do whatever you can to make this a special space, so you feel comfortable enough to stay a while and go deep.

WHAT ARE THE PAYOFFS OF STAYING STUCK?

Before we move on to the next assignment, which is slaying your inner kraken (I'll explain what this is in a little bit), it's important to realize that there are pay-offs to being stuck in our beliefs, even if they hurt us. You won't be able to move forward until you see what your subconscious pay-offs are, so you can consciously challenge them, forgive yourself and let them go. Here are a few of the benefits of staying stuck in your beliefs:

◆ You get to avoid change, responsibility, love, success, visibility, vulnerability.

◆ You get to feel more powerful by failing, thus punishing those you don't think loved you enough.

◆ You get to feel righteous, complaining to everyone about the person you believe inspired guilt, anger or hurt in you, rather than expressing your honest emotion to that person and give them the chance to address it or prove you might have gotten it wrong.

◆ You want a guarantee before making a change.

◆ You want to manipulate others with self-pity. If they see you as a victim or noble sufferer, then they will help you make your life work.

◆ You get to feel better than others, feeling entitled to special treatment because of your suffering.

◆ You're afraid your success will make you lose control, friends, attention, excuses, invisibility, safety of mediocrity, etc.

Please don't make this an opportunity to judge yourself. Forgive yourself and gently choose new beliefs based in self-honesty, courage and love. You are much more powerful than you give yourself credit for!

EXERCISE 2A: WHAT DOES MY INNER
KRAKEN TELL ME?

Okay, get ready because we're gonna release the kraken—that big monster inside you that believes the worst things about you and relishes reminding you about your shortcomings. For those of you who didn't see "Clash of the Titans," there is a giant sea monster in Greek Mythology with epic strength called a Kraken, whose tentacles could pull entire ships down into the depths of the ocean and destroy cities. It also boasted a gaping maw full of many sharp teeth. To me, our negative inner voice—what many psychologists call the inner saboteur—looks like a kraken because it hides underneath the dark waters of our subconscious and rises to destroy without warning.

You can absolutely slay the kraken, but not in the traditional action movie sense. You see, the kraken can't be killed. Sometimes the kraken is there to help you fight. It's just that you need to harness its power when you need it and tell it to be quiet when its fury does not serve you.

How does that sound? Don't worry, we're not gonna do any trauma therapy here. We don't need to heal everything. We just want to do a ritual that lets the kraken know it's no longer in charge. It will still be there, but tamed, and you can harness that energy and channel it in a healthier way. This enables a more loving voice to take the stage. As the famous drag queen RuPaul says in his reality television series "RuPaul's Drag Race," the negative voice will always be there, so you must counteract it with a stronger, more empowered one.

Do the Exercise 2A: What Does My Inner Kraken Tell Me? Worksheet on the facing page, using these instructions: Write down ALL the reasons people—or your own self—said you didn't quite fit in, or measure up, through your whole life. Sometimes the bad things we say to ourselves we wouldn't dream of saying to another person. If you're not sure about this, a good place to start is to think about the people whom you compare yourself to and believe are better than you in some way. As Theodore Roosevelt said, "Comparison is the thief of joy."

You may feel like doing this a few times until it feels finished. It doesn't mean all the bad thoughts disappear, but rather you feel a sense of relief that you've exposed what's needed for now. We just want to shine the light on the dark corners in your mind so that they hold less power over you.

Get it all down until it feels complete—for now. I'd like to uncover at least 10 that bother you the most, but feel free to add more if you like now or later as they come up.

When you have taken a break please do Exercise 2B: Release the Kraken's Hold on the next page, using the instructions below:

EXERCISE 2A: WHAT DOES MY KRAKEN TELL ME?

1

2

3

4

5

6

7

8

9

10

EXAMPLES: I am lazy. I am always late. I am ugly. I am fat. I am not good enough.

EXERCISE 2B: DISCREDIT THE INNER KRAKEN

What does my kraken tell me?	
Negative thoughts from 2A	Evidence it isn't true
1	
2	
3	
4	
5	
6	
7	
8	
9	
10	
11	
12	

We're going to formally go through the process of looking for evidence that these negative thoughts identified in Exercise 2A aren't true. This is a good way to challenge the negative beliefs and see that they don't really define you. When I did this process myself, I felt much lighter!

In the worksheet's "Evidence this Isn't True" column, write down the reasons why you know the judgments weren't deserved or choose a more positive way to frame it, so it loses its negative charge and feels better. Here are some examples to get you started:

◆ If someone frequently called you lazy, and there were times where you might have been, look for evidence of times where you weren't lazy.

◆ If someone called you ugly, remind yourself of times when people acknowledged things that were beautiful about you, such as your eyes, your smile, your style, or your inner beauty.

◆ If someone called you fat, and you were overweight, look for a healthier description to show this negative judgment meant to shame you isn't true. Maybe think of yourself as "big and beautiful" or remember times when you felt or were called sexy. The goal here is to reframe your thinking so it doesn't become a reason to harm your self-esteem. Remember, I attracted my soul mate at 300 pounds, but I had learned to feel sexy, which made me more magnetic.

RELEASE THE KRAKEN RITUAL

Now it's time to officially free this inner beast so it isn't taking up so much space in your head and heart. Take your time and have fun with it!

I've provided a couple of exercises to help you with this process, and you may come up with a creative idea of your own. It doesn't really matter what the ritual is—it's all about setting your intention and putting your inner beast on notice!

EXERCISE: THE MOVIE IN YOUR MIND

Please read through the instructions of this visualization exercise and then do it on your own, at your own pace, with each of the negative beliefs from the previous assignments.

◆ Take the first negative belief about yourself that you'd like to address and close your eyes. Take three deep, slow, cleansing breaths and imagine yourself enveloped by a warm cocoon of golden, protective light.

◆ See the words in your mind's eye, and think back to the first time you can remember thinking this thought. If you don't remember the first time, just think back to whatever time that thought disturbed you.

◆ From a more detached, curious place, as if you were watching a movie about someone else, allow yourself to see scenes—memories—associated with this thought. These can be memories of someone telling you this thought, or a time you simply remember thinking it. If it's a bit challenging at first to stay objective, call in your higher power to amplify your protective cocoon.

◆ If at any time you start to feel emotional, just gently notice it and allow yourself to detach again as it if were happening to someone else.

◆ Ask yourself, is it possible that any of this perceived criticism was delivered by someone who intended to help you grow or protect you? Was this person projecting their own fears on to you? Sometimes we must overlook the inept delivery and listen to the message.

◆ If this a "yes" for you, use your imagination and see yourself back in the situation. Putting your emotions and insecurities aside, imagine the person delivering the message in a more constructive and loving way so that you could receive it better, and more objectively decide if it applies to you. If it's your own negative thought, perhaps it was just a part if you that intended to keep you safe.

◆ Imagine yourself receiving it now from a higher perspective and thank the messenger, forgiving them and yourself for any judgment. Our flaws are a part of us, but they do *not* define us. Sometimes our flaws can even be our superpowers, because we can help others who struggle with the same thing.

◆ If it's something that still needs addressing, such

as you're often late, promise yourself that you will do the work, starting today, to address it, even if it is a baby step like buying a book about it. Vow to yourself you will no longer allow this to be a reason to ding your self-worth.

◆ If what was said is untrue, remind yourself that most of the ugly things said to us that we are still carrying inside us are total hogwash. Sometimes these things are said by miserable people who subconsciously learned to feel bigger by making others feel small. Or maybe they were insecure, and you triggered jealousy in them. Or maybe they weren't even thinking when they said it and didn't mean any harm.

◆ Take a moment to really see that from a more objective place. Call on your higher power to feel compassion for those who dented your self-esteem and forgive them.

◆ Most importantly, forgive yourself for believing you are not perfectly imperfect exactly as you are. Promise yourself you will focus more on your positive traits. Say, "I forgive myself and those who have harmed me. I understand that these experiences have made me stronger and I will seek the lesson or the higher purpose they awaken within me."

◆ See yourself lovingly take an eraser and wipe away the negative thought. Based on your evidence that it isn't true. Replace it with a more positive thought that you can buy into in this moment. Allow any positive feelings that arise from thinking a more loving thought to arise.

When you are done with the list, you may choose to discard it with a small ritual.

RITUAL OPTIONS

Do it in whatever way feels right here. It's just about symbolically releasing it. One option is to lovingly see your higher power surround that list in a ball of light and taking it away so it harms no one. Or maybe flushing that list down the toilet feels gleefully good? How about ripping it into shreds and safely torching them in a burning bowl ceremony?

I love the idea of crumbling it into a ball, stomping on it and channeling Rhett Butler from "Gone with the Wind." I think it would be satisfying to give the paper a kick and say, "Frankly my dear I don't give a damn what you think!"

Whatever way you want to purge, go for it. I don't judge, and neither should you. Purge like no one is watching. Or purge like they are watching but their opinions are their own darned business. Just keep it in a place of fun and empowerment rather than bitterness and you're on the right track!

If you are feeling anger, it is actually a good sign if you have been sad or depressed. Each emotion we feel has a certain energetic vibration. The more negative the emotion, like depression and despair, the lower the vibration. The highest vibration we can experience is through love. In law of attraction, anger is a higher vibration than depression, so it means you are lifting yourself out of that darkest of emotional states. Psychotherapists agree with that point, saying it means that your fighting spirit is reawakening.

I don't want you to stay stuck in anger though. The goal is to forgive yourself for allowing your internal and external negative forces to have a strong hold on you.

If declaring your how great the release felt online would feel empowering and reinforcing, feel free to post it on my Facebook page @*mysoulmatecoach*, and not only will our online community support you, but it can inspire others who need to draw their line in the sand with the haters out there. If this feels right to you, please be careful not to mention any specific private details. You may also ask any questions about the process and I will give you feedback.

If you need a little help with the meditation/visualization part of it, you can find my "forgiveness" video on my Facebook page and website *www.mysoulmatecoach.com*.

The point is to begin the process of letting go of the inaccurate judgments you've taken on, in whatever way feels right in this moment. Everyone is in a different place in their process. Wherever you are, start now so you can transform and get what you want all the faster.

You deserve it!

ASSIGNMENT 2C: WHY YOU ROCK
After a break, let's continue the process of becoming more magnetic to our soul mate(s)—and our ideal life—by starting to put more focus on what's right in our lives. As Oprah said, "What you focus on expands, and when you focus on the goodness in

your life, you create more of it." If you need help getting started, ask a loved one to tell you what they see.

Let's do this! Go to the next page and dig into Exercise 2C: Tell the World Why You Rock! If you like, hang up the sheet in a place you can see it daily, so it reminds you about how fabulous you are. Then take another break and return here.

If you'd like to sit with this feeling of self-positivity you get from doing the exercise, feel free to do the "I Have Value" guided meditation on *www.MySoulMateCoach.com*!

Then I recommend that you take a long break—at least a day—to integrate these new thoughts and get in the habit of shifting your old negative thoughts as they arise and refocusing to your positive new beliefs. This is something that will get easier with time but takes some discipline. Paying more attention to your thoughts, and actively shifting them to more constructive ones is a new habit, but it's well worth the effort. Spending more time thinking about what's *right* about you, instead of what's supposedly wrong, will make you feel lighter, and more like your true self.

WHY YOU'RE STILL SINGLE: YOUR INTUITION KNOWS THE PATTERNS THAT KEEP YOU STUCK

If you're still reading this book, then you have probably started to accept the notion that part of the reason you are single is you. I mean this with love, as I've been in your shoes, but it's important to be honest so I can help fast track your transformation. You are in good company, as many people struggle with this.

The problem is not really them, but that's the exciting part. Realizing it is you is deliciously empowering. It's a gift when you

EXERCISE 2C: TELL THE WORLD WHY YOU ROCK!

Positive thought	Evidence it is true
1	
2	
3	
4	
5	
6	
7	
8	
9	
10	
11	
12	

understand and own this, because you are something you can change—starting right now in this moment if you choose.

Thinking that you are at the mercy of a small, toxic dating pool in a dark, cruel world makes you feel completely powerless. Buying into that type of thinking only trains your brain to look for more evidence of that "truth," which if you can't find it, you will subconsciously create that scenario. If you have a dating pattern you can't shake, then you know in your heart that this is true.

You don't have to be a fan of "Sex and the City" to relate to this universal storyline. In one of my favorite scenes of the show, a celebrity therapist asks Carrie—who is obsessed with her commitment-phobic ex-boyfriend—if she typically dates men who can't give her what she needs. Carrie shrugs it off like it's just the bad luck of dating in the city. The therapist points out that the one thing the men all have in common is Carrie, who scoffs and proceeds to date a fellow therapy patient. He was played by Jon Bon Jovi, so who could blame her? However, after a night of passion, her date withdraws, admitting that he's in therapy because he completely loses interest in women after sex. Carrie realizes, to her chagrin, that this is a breakthrough moment and admits that she unconsciously picks the wrong men.

Now, you may still be feeling a little bit of resistance to this idea. That's okay. Just stay with me because I will show you the way out of this mental trap so you can get out of your own way.

You may be used to telling your friends—and yourself—that each person you have dated has been different so it can't be that you choose the wrong men or women. One was a stockbroker, while another was an artist, and another owned a consulting business. Their personalities were different, and you broke up for different reasons. You've said they were not reflective of anything unresolved with your mother or father. You have done too much work on yourself and are too spiritually evolved to be such a textbook case. Sound familiar?

But the one thing they had in common is that they all seemed great at first, and then the dark side came out. The circumstances and the issues were different on the surface, and yet each one evoked the same feeling of disappointment or grief. The feeling of history repeating itself.

The key to taking the next step is to use your intuition to see that there is indeed a pattern—and it will stay a pattern until you learn whatever lesson it is trying to teach you. Perhaps you are like Carrie and you keep dating people who can't give you what you need. Is it possible that your subconscious is picking people to help you resolve something from the past? Putting aside any internal resistance to sounding like a cliché, was there a parent who couldn't accept you or show love? Did your past romantic prospects in some way try to change you or withhold love? Did you perhaps stay way too long, bending yourself into a pretzel to find evidence that this person accepted you or would show love eventually—once you figured out how to get them to see you?

The truth is, and this is a big one, that each of these people were just a mirror for how you saw yourself, how you felt about yourself at the time. The ones who come in the future are going to keep mirroring until you learn that the love you are seeking from outside is something that must come from within. You must accept yourself—warts and all—and show yourself wholehearted love. You may still be thinking you are the exception, but trust me, there is a pattern and a lesson that, until acknowledged, will keep on hurting and disappointing you, making you so discouraged you sometimes want to give up.

In my case, my father was mentally ill, which led him to be violent, verbally cruel and emotionally unavailable. He ignored me completely. As a child I didn't understand he was a tortured person working two jobs with an untreated mental disorder. I just thought I wasn't loveable enough to gain his attention. I shut it behind a thick door in my heart and denied it was there, throwing myself into my marketing career and friends.

While the work side was going better than I could have imagined, the part of me that wanted a mate was lost. I started pining for unavailable men from afar, not seeing the ones who wanted me. If they gave me any reason to think they might like me, I would stay stuck in that fantasy for a while until it blew up in my face. At times I would see this fear of intimacy and feel embarrassment, but I would suppress it with a pint of Haagen Daaz.

After much therapy, as well as 12-step work, I made sure to pick men who were physically gentle. I told myself this was evidence that I was too evolved to be repeating my relationship with my dad. But in truth every man I picked was emotionally unavailable and feared intimacy. On the surface they seemed kind, but when I started to seek emotional support, they shut down and sometimes said cruel things to push me away. They initially pursued me, which was intoxicating to me, and then ran or pushed me away when I expected a relationship. When I would start to move on, they would appear again and woo me, starting the cycle again.

Although I couldn't see it, deep down I blamed myself, thinking there was something wrong with me. Owning up to this pattern shined the light on how I subconsciously didn't believe I deserved better. They were a mirror for my own fear of intimacy. My reality simply reflected this belief because I kept creating it.

I invite you to chew on that thought and do some reflecting. Maybe take a nature walk or meditate upon it. If you're having trouble getting started, here is a worksheet to help give you clues on what your pattern(s) might be.

Once you are simply aware of the pattern, then you can immediately shift and won't be doomed to repeating it. Once that occurs, the key will be to keep reminding yourself that you get it now and you don't have to keep expecting history to repeat itself. Now you can begin the journey of expecting something better.

Now rub your hands together gleefully, because we're about to get to the bottom of what your patterns are. Together we will discover—with curiosity rather than punishment—what resistance is there to attracting what you want. Once that is cleared away, it is much easier to get clarity on your ideal mate and truly understand you deserve that relationship.

WHAT ARE YOUR RELATIONSHIP PATTERNS?
Below are some exercises to help you figure out what your patterns are. Before you start, I invite you to get into your beautiful, inspired and quiet space and take these on like a detective working a case – detached and curious. There is nothing to fear or feel shame about. Many "strong" people got to that place by making

mistakes. Getting clarity is key to moving on and getting your greatest good. If you feel any negativity, just gently notice it and detach again with an air of curiosity. Got it? Go for it.

Simply reflect on the people you've dated, or wanted to date, and put down why it didn't work out. Once it feels complete, I'll ask you to review it again and we'll look at it through another lens.

Ready to be a detective? We are going to solve this. You may get it all in one sitting or it may come in stages. It's all okay. It's all about opening the trap door and letting the light in.

EXERCISE 2D: WHAT ARE YOUR EMOTIONAL PATTERNS IN RELATIONSHIPS?

Please do Exercises 2D-2F on the following pages.

Take a break and return when you are ready!

And now on to Exercise 2G. **Look at the Relationship Patterns listed in Exercise 2G: Common Relationship Patterns** and consider how your unresolved relationships could have driven them. Please do not rush this. Really sit and look.

If you feel a sense of discomfort or denial when you read any of them, that's a strong signal this may apply to you. The key is to allow yourself to look at it like a detective—with curiosity and detachment—and if any thoughts of self-judgment or discomfort arise, just gently notice those and use those feelings to identify which of these are true for you. Tap into a feeling of gratitude for these emotions, for they are direct communiques from your intuition. Rather than avoid or dwell on the discomfort, just gently notice it and detach into a more curious space.

Circle the ones that seem true for you, and when you are

done, journal what you learned and take a break. Then return here and read the introduction to the Exercise 2H: Identifying More Negative Relationship Patterns Worksheet.

EXERCISE 2H: OWNING MY RELATIONSHIP PATTERNS WITHOUT JUDGMENT

Another way you can look at your relationship patterns is to ask yourself these questions:

◆ Do I keep dating my father/mother or keep finding the same person (even if they appear different at the beginning)?

◆ What NEGATIVE qualities seem persistent in the people I date?

◆ Do I tend to get triggered in relationships by certain words or behaviors used by my partners? If so, what are the triggers and how do I react to them?

When you reflect on your answers, get quiet and gently ask your intuition if there is major unresolved trauma from your childhood that needs healing. If you don't think you can heal it on your own, consider seeking counseling or a support group. If the pattern is based on false beliefs, you simply must let those go and replace them with a new belief. If it's something that you can shift on your own through self-care and awareness, please do so.

Once you have some thoughts on what your patterns are, do 2H worksheet on page 77. You might revisit it again later if more insights come into awareness. Once 2H feels complete,

TEXT CONTINUED ON PAGE 78S

The Soul Mate Coach

EXERCISE 2D: WHAT'S YOUR EMOTIONAL PATTERN IN RELATIONSHIPS?

Briefly jot down key words and phrases to describe your feelings and beliefs about the relationships/prospects below. See emotions list in panel opposite if you need help.

A	Name of Ex-Partner or Prospect I Didn't Date
B	What initially attracted me to this person? What words best describe the top qualities that attracted you?
C	What main emotions did you feel when you started dating? OR What main emotions did you feel as you imagined dating this person?
D	What primary emotions did you feel most in the relationship (if you dated)? OR How did it feel to want this person and not date them?

E	Why did you break up? OR Why didn't it pan out?
F	What main emotions did you feel when the relationship ended, or the prospect didn't pan out?

EMOTIONS	
Fear	Disappointment
Grief	Overwhelm
Depression	Frustration
Despair	Boredom
Powerlessness	Relief
Unworthiness	Contentment
Jealousy	Hopefulness
Insecurity	Optimism
Guilt	Positive Expectation/Belief
Hatred/Rage/Revenge	Enthusiasm/Eagerness/Happiness
Anger/Blame	Passion
Discouragement	Joy/Empowerment/Freedom
Worry	Appreciation/Gratitude
Doubt	Love

EXERCISE 2E: WHAT'S YOUR EMOTIONAL PATTERN?

Briefly jot down the words that came up most in the chart above

What 3 qualities attracted me the most in previous relationships and Prospects?	What 3 emotions did I feel most in early dating or desiring the person?	What main 3 emotions did I feel most of the time when dating this person or when imagining dating them?	What are the top 3 reasons these relationships didn't work out and who initiated the end?	What are the 3 main emotions did you feel when the relationship ended, or the prospect didn't pan out?
1	1	1	1	1
2	2	2	2	2
3	3	3	3	3

The Soul Mate Coach

EXERCISE 2F: WHAT'S YOUR EMOTIONAL PATTERN

Questions for Reflection and Journaling**

When looking at column C above, what person(s) did you feel these emotions within your childhood or teen years?

When looking at column E above, what person(s) did you feel these emotions within your childhood or teen years?

When reflecting on your current relationship with this person(s) is it the way you would like it to be? If not, what is unresolved?

** Please note if this was a physical, sexual or emotionally abusive relationship, it is recommended you discuss this with a therapist.

If not resolved, and from a place of detached curiosity, what do you think are the primary reasons this person harmed you, whether intentionally or unintentionally? Was it their:

◆ Fear?

◆ Dishonesty?

◆ Selfishness?

◆ ack of awareness?

If you were to look at this as a detached adult, is it possible they did the best they could at their stage of emotional/spiritual development? If so, how could that change the way you see them?

From a place of detached curiosity, what responsibility** can you take in this discord without punishing yourself? Was it partly due to your own:

◆ Fear?

◆ Dishonesty?

◆ Selfishness?

◆ Lack of awareness?

WORKSHEET CONTINUED NEXT PAGE

If you were to look at this relationship from a soul level:

What lesson did you learn—about yourself and others—from this discord?

What action can you take to come to peace with it?

Examples:

◆ Would you be willing to forgive them for their part in the discord?

◆ Would you be willing to forgive yourself?

◆ Would you be willing to give yourself the love/acceptance you need moving forward?

The Soul Mate Coach

EXERCISE 2G: RELATIONSHIP PATTERNS

Below are common relationship pattern themes. Please review for reflection and uncovering what feels true for you so you can become aware and move on. Circle the ones that fit.**

Theme	Emotional cues
Codependence	◆ I obsessively need to take care of others.
	◆ I need to control the actions of others.
	◆ I have trouble setting/respecting boundaries.
	◆ I'm a people pleaser and feel taken advantage of.
	◆ I lose myself or give too much.
	◆ My needs come last in relationships.
	◆ I fear rejection if I say no.
	◆ I depend too much on other's opinions.
	◆ I become too involved in other's problems or rescuing others.
	◆ I tend to attract partners with addictions.
	◆ I avoid intimacy and close relationships because I am afraid of any or all the above.
Control	◆ I tend to seek partners who will tell me what to do so I don't have to take responsibility.
	◆ I tend to blame partners for my shortcomings.
	◆ I tend to seek partners who don't take responsibility for their word or actions.
	◆ I tend to seek partners whom I can control so I feel safe.

WORKSHEET CONTINUED NEXT PAGE

Dependence	◆ I tend to seek partners who will take care of me financially or emotionally. ◆ I over-rely on others to meet my physical and emotional needs.
Conflict	◆ I tend to avoid or seek conflict in relationships. ◆ I tend to feel high anxiety in relationships. ◆ I tend to be defensive in conflict. ◆ I tend to be judgmental in relationships. ◆ I have trouble communicating my truth for fear of retaliation. ◆ I tend to hold my feelings in until I explode (rage) or implode (addiction). ◆ I often blame partners for my failures or holding me back. ◆ I tend to be passive aggressive or attract passive aggressive partners. ◆ I tend to be aggressive or disrespectful when things don't go the way I think they should, or I feel insecure. ◆ I tend to attract partners who are often aggressive or disrespectful when they don't get what they want. ◆ The quality of friendships and frequency of getting together has decreased when I'm in relationships. ◆ I obsess over what was said/not said.

**If any of these patterns feel deep, consistent, obsessive or overwhelming patterns resulting from trauma, please consider therapy that can precede this journey or run alongside it. While coaches can be extremely valuable in helping clients transform, they are not trained counselors for healing trauma or diagnosing mental health issues.

Fear of abandonment	◆ I attract partners who can't express or give love.
	◆ I stay in relationships too long because I need to show a return on my investment.
	◆ I stay in relationships too long because deep down I am unsure I can do better.
	◆ I attract partners who can't commit or leave me.
	◆ I can't commit in relationships because I fear being engulfed or abandoned.
Fear of intimacy	◆ I tend to overly romanticize or idealize relationships and partners.
	◆ I tend to be dishonest or secretive in relationships because I don't think people would love the real me.
	◆ I tend to be dishonest or secretive in relationships because I don't think I can get my needs met by speaking my truth.
	◆ I tend to be inauthentic/can't relax in relationships because I'm afraid I'm unlovable.
	◆ I often find myself posing so I look attractive with partners.
	◆ I often feel self-conscious in relationships, trying to act the way I think my partner wants because I fear they will leave.
	◆ I feel empowered around immature or less evolved partners.
	◆ I avoid or feel insecure around confident partners who might challenge me.

WORKSHEET CONTINUED NEXT PAGE

Fear of intimacy (contd.)	◆ I avoid or feel insecure around confident partners who might challenge me.
	◆ I tend to compare myself to potentially healthy partners and feel lacking or unworthy.
	◆ I don't feel I deserve my ideal partner.
	◆ I have trust issues.
	◆ I'm sexually insatiable.
	◆ I have a history of unstable relationships.
	◆ I explode when I am angry or have trouble expressing emotions.
Abusive	If you attract people who physically and verbally abuse you, please seek professional counseling. You must face and release the trauma from this before you can shift this. This book will be here when you are ready.

What did I learn about myself after reviewing these? Use this space for any journaling you want to do.

EXERCISE 2H: OWNING MY PATTERNS WITHOUT JUDGMENT

Relationship Patterns I See Now

How Might My Early Relationships Caused These Patterns

Moving How May I Learn and Let it Go in a Responsible, Loving Way?

What Steps am I Willing to Take Now to Move Forward?

please put down your pen or pencil and celebrate! This is a major step in your shift, and your bravery will be rewarded.

MARK A MAJOR MILESTONE IN YOUR SOUL MATE MAGNETIZING SHIFT!

To make sure you truly salute the work you have done, I invite you to do an *extra* act of self-care *today*. Do something you normally don't take the time to do that makes you feel good. Some ideas:

◆ Take a bath with candles

◆ Do arts and crafts.

◆ Make a vision board.

◆ Take a day trip or walk on your favorite trail.

◆ Go to the movies or a museum.

◆ Bake or cook something delicious.

◆ Get a spa treatment or go to the beauty salon.

◆ Read a book just for fun.

◆ Go dancing or dance in your living room.

Whatever you do, please do it TODAY instead of putting off pleasure. It's one of the most important parts of your shift. If you feel moved to, please share your insights, questions and self-care ideas in the Soul Mate Magnetizers group on Facebook *@MySoulMateCoach* so we can support you!

BUST RELATIONSHIP MYTHS THAT KEEP YOU STUCK
One of the reasons we stay blocked—especially those who arrive at mid-life without a soul mate—is because we buy into societal myths that make for humorous comments in movies and television but are false.

There are many, but for the purpose of brevity, we will focus on the main three myths I hear from clients:

1. All the Good Ones are Taken

Instead of focusing on the experience of you and your friends, which is impacted by so many variables, including fear-based beliefs, it's best to focus on the facts. From a purely statistical standpoint, there are so many singles—of all age groups. We've been trained to believe in a "lack" mentality, but it is a way to blame lack of success on external factors instead of owning our part in the situation. The truth is, there is an abundance of singles out there, in part because they are waiting to marry longer. I only have access to U.S. stats, but it gives a good perspective no matter where you are based. There are:

- 124.6 million adult singles in America, representing over 50% of all US residents.

- 77% of singles are aged 35+

From a subjective standpoint, some people get entrenched in this belief because they think that the qualities they are looking for are hard to find. In my experience, this is simply not true, but it feels true because some clients have unrealistic expectations. They want everything on their list, or they claim they are settling. The truth is, it's not possible to get everything on your list from one person. Clinging to that belief is a way I believe some people justify not putting themselves out there.

Instead of looking at it as "settling" I invite you to look at it as not putting all your emotional needs in one basket. No one person is going to be perfectly compatible with you. If you can see this objectively as an adult, you'll see that waiting for a unicorn is a great way to be lonely. In keeping with the philosophy that you can't appreciate the light without darkness, it's wise to see that a 100% harmonious relationship would be boring and not inspire any growth in you. It is the conflict and struggle we face in relationships that gives us the resistance we need to evolve.

I felt great relief early in my marriage when we went to a seminar developed by renowned relationship expert John Gottman, who authored the New York Times bestseller, "The Seven Principles for Making Marriage Work." He did decades of research which showed that 69 percent of relationship conflict is about perpetual problems, so we should let go of the high expectation that everything can be "fixed." You can manage the relationship differences so that you can live as peacefully as possible, but there will always be things about your partner you wish were different. I invite you to respect these differences because without them life would be boring and wouldn't inspire you to grow.

Not everything should be about "equal" responsibility as that is a trap. Constantly keeping score is another great way to stay alone. It's about each partner taking on responsibility based on their strengths, so that the partnership thrives. Once I came to see and accept that, I felt a lot of judgment and frustration melt away, and I could start to see I was supported in the way my partner could support me. I share this with you because many of my single clients are so frightened about being taken advantage of that they are constantly keeping score from the first date. They think all the "perfect guys" who support their partners equitably are married to lucky women and make it impossible for a "great guy" in front of them who wants to please them.

For many clients, something that keeps them entrenched in the false belief that the "good ones are taken," is what I call "aspirational dating." They are looking to trade up—almost like they are shopping for a luxury item they can't afford—so they stay in a state of waiting for an elusive prince who is never coming.

Many clients initially resist what I am about to say, because it isn't very romantic, and it can sound harsh. However, it really isn't harsh. It's just a reality check some singles need in modern dating. If the average person were to rate themselves objectively on a scale of one to 10 as a total package—personality, looks, career success, wealth, spirituality, health, etc.—they would be around a 5. Average is NOT bad, but we are taught to think it's sub-par. Some daters take this concept so seriously that they won't settle for anything less than "perfection" and they wind up lonely. When many people stay stuck in unrealistic expectations, it's often because they have a low self-esteem, and are looking to find validation in a quest for a princess or princess who isn't coming.

It's not their fault, either. How many movies do we see where the chubby, awkward nerd obsesses over the "perfect 10" cheerleader and wins her in the end? Or how many romance novels have an average girl next door capture the attention of a movie star and win his heart? How many people watched "50 Shades of Grey" and watched wistfully as a college senior won the love of a hot twenty-something millionaire. I called it "50 Shades of Wrong" because there is no universe where this is realistically happening.

It's a lovely fantasy but in this regard, Hollywood is doing us no favors. When I was dating online in my late 30s, I was "fluffy," pretty and well known in my field. I thought of myself as a "6" and perhaps a "7." I wasn't a supermodel and I wasn't looking for one. I was matched on several occasions to balding, overweight, and moderately successful Silicon Valley nerds whom I would have considered "in my league," but they wouldn't even look at me. On one particular dating site, you had to pick your top 10 "must haves" from a drop-down list and every single one of these men chose "my mate must be considered extremely attractive by most social standards" and "my mate must be wealthy." In other words, they were looking for someone like swimsuit model Chrissy Teigen, who was never looking for an "average" or even "above average" guy. She was looking for someone like John Legend to marry in a Lake Como Italy luxury villa!

I know many of you are nodding your heads because you have experienced this sort of rejection because some people have very unrealistic expectations. The truth is, a "5" or a "6" or even a "7" is leaving themselves open to a lot of unnecessary pain by pining for a "10." Of course, it's possible that a "10" might go on a date with them but they are not likely going to be satisfied and stay. They will hold out for other "10s" for various reasons—and not necessarily shallow ones. I'm not a fan of the expression "dating out of your league" because it implies the person one person is not good enough. My point is, a "5" dating a "10" is not likely going to feel secure, or feel like they measure up, which does not lead to being themselves and feeling happy. If they instead date someone who is closer to their "level" as a package, both partners have a better chance of being satisfied, secure and appreciated for their authentic selves. A "10" might feel like they could do better, and if their ego is unchecked might actually say so to their "average" partner, which is not a recipe for relationship success.

I know some folks reading this will be looking furiously for the loophole, and in my opinion as a relationship coach, there are two possible ones. In one scenario, if the "average" part-ner was extremely humble in their self-rating and the "10" per-ceived them as much closer to their "score," it could work. If the self-assessed "average" person is attracting a lot of "9s" and 10s" that that could very well be the case. I don't think that is very common though, based on my coaching and personal ex-periences. The other loophole is in the old-fashioned gold-digger or gigolo scenario, and while that arrangement might work for some, I don't think that's what you are looking for!

If you're fuming right now reading this, I get it. No one wants to hear it. It can sound to some as unromantic and cynical. But my goal here is to end the suffering that comes from having such high expectations that they can never be satisfied with someone great who appreciates them. Having the mindset of searching for the "best" instead of "good enough" often leads to anxiety, dissatisfaction, and pain. We are often taught that having more choices is empowering and offer more opportunities to get the "best" product. But research shows that an excess of choices often leads us to be less satisfied when we decide on a product, because there is often the fear that we could have done better. I do believe that people often get stuck in this "shopping for the best" mindset and it becomes counterproductive. They become overwhelmed and paralyzed by the options, sometimes overlooking a "product" they would have been happy with but were afraid something better might come along.

I want you to be happy. I want you to be with someone who is a great match and loves and appreciates you AS YOU ARE NOW. And you feel the same about them. It's important to have that going for you because relationships are HARD. When conflict arises, many people fear that they made the "wrong" choice and missed out on "something better." If this is something that you have experienced, it is very common. I'm saying this with love because I believe you will never be happy if you don't let his go.

Here's the good news. If you're not happy with dating people "in your league," then my best advice is to work on yourself as a total package and raise your score. You can do that. That's why this book is called "Be the Soul Mate You Want to Attract." Become a better version of you so you can date someone you can be satisfied with—and they you!

2. I'm Not Good Enough

Most people struggle with this to some extent, and it's often unconscious. You'll know this is true for you if, when you think of going on a date, you're more worried about whether the person finds you appealing rather than evaluating their viability as a soul mate. Along the way, life experience has caused us to forget that we are all beautiful. We are all enough.

The easiest way to remember you are good enough is to *stop comparing yourself to others.*

Author Paul Angone said it well, when he wrote, "Obsessive Comparison Disorder is a phrase I've coined to describe our compulsion to constantly compare ourselves with others, producing unwanted thoughts and feelings that drive us to depression, consumption, anxiety, and all-around joyous discontent."

When I coach clients in dating or career, they are often hindered—sometimes crippled—by basing their value on how they measure up to others. Don't do that. Instead, replace that compulsion with a new one:

◆ Put on Blinders by Shifting Your Focus—When you find yourself comparing yourself to others, shift your focus on what you do well and how you make a difference in people's lives.

◆ Cut Social Media & TV in Half and Amp Up the Self-Care—Social media and television are fabulous in small doses, but too much can cause you to think the grass is greener in everyone else's lives. Instead, love yourself more by filling up your tanks with self-care, from pampering and healthy eating to exercise, time outdoors, reading or learning something new.

◆ Celebrate Accomplishments—When you do something well, or receive recognition, say thank you instead of explaining it away. Take time to mark every milestone—large or small—because it's a good reminder that *you* made this happen.

If you'd like more support in shifting this, check out the "I Have Value" meditation on my website.

3. I'll Lose Myself

It's very common for people to fear they will lose themselves in a relationship, but with awareness and clarity, the opposite will happen with a soul mate. A soul mate will help you remember more layers of who you really are.

If you tend to put relationships first, posing in relationships or believe you can't find someone who accepts you or inspires you to grow, then losing yourself is likely.

The cures for this are:

◆ Establish a strong foundation while you are single.

◆ Know who you are, who you aren't and be authentic.

◆ Establish strong boundaries and communicate.

◆ Have your own interests and friends.

◆ Stop over giving and accommodating.

SHIFTING FALSE BELIEFS THAT BLOCK HEALTHY RELATIONSHIPS

Let's look at some other dating and relationship beliefs that may be blocking your ability to attract and maintain a healthy relationship. Do any of these apply to you?

- The "right" relationship should "just work."

- I can change another person if they love me or I love them enough.

- It's normal to yell at my partner (or other relative/ friend) from time to time—it shows I really love them.

- Lots of relationship drama is just part of life.

- There is only "the one."

- Everyone basically experiences love the same way.

- The relationships I saw growing up do not affect my relationships today.

- I expect men/women in relationships to behave a certain way.

When it comes to relationship myths, we all have them to some extent. If you answered "yes" to any of these, here are some thoughts to help you shift these beliefs:

The "right" relationship should just organically work without a lot of effort or conflict.

As discussed earlier, even soul mate relationships take conscious effort, and often push our buttons so we can grow. There will be times of both harmony and stress in even the greatest loves. As John Gottman pointed out, all couples have these ongoing incompatibilities — even if they appear "perfect" on social media—because they arise from fundamental differences. According to Gottman, these are either fundamental differences in your personalities that repeatedly cause conflict, or fundamental differences in your lifestyle needs. They are paradoxes to be managed rather than problems to be solved.

For this reason, it's really important to let go of any notion that the ideal relationship won't have conflict. I have had clients who grew up with parents who "were always happy" and "never fought" and are perplexed because their partner seems to "enjoy conflict." Any marriage counselor will tell you that conflict, if handled respectfully with respect to each other's boundaries, is important for deepening intimacy. When couples don't ever argue, they are usually both avoiding conflict because they are afraid of confrontation or worry that it will harm their bond. Sometimes lack of conflict can also signal a lack of passion in the relationship. Is it any wonder that the always harmonious June and Ward Cleaver in the 1960s sitcom "Leave it to Beaver" had separate beds?

I'll give you an example of how I learned that I should allow conflict rather than avoid it in relationships. As you'll see a bit later in this section, I discovered what I really needed in my ideal soul mate relationship because my previous relationship lacked it and caused me pain.

One of the things that relationship lacked was open conflict. We were both conflicted inside for various reasons but avoiding expressing it because we were not honoring our boundaries and being authentic. The truth was, this was a relationship of comfort and convenience, but not passion. When I met my husband, I had to confront my fear of conflict.

For those who enjoy astrology, I am a typical Cancer in that I find disagreements stressful and by nature take it personally, so

I hold onto it. My husband is a typical Aries in that he has no trouble fighting at all, and when he's done blowing up, he lets it go and moves on.

When a friend who was more devoted to astrology than I was pointed out that a Cancer/Aries relationship was doomed to failure, I ignored it. I noticed that I seemed to be attracting a lot of Aries into my life—not only my husband but also my stepson and three dear friends—and I believed there was a reason for that. I realized that I was way too sensitive, and that I could learn to take things less personally and not get so threatened about conflict. I in turn helped the Aries in my life become more choosey about what really needed to be a battle and what didn't, and how to soften their approach.

Ultimately, we've helped balance each other out, which is a good thing. It's not always easy for either of us, but we've grown from it. My previous partner was a Cancer like myself, and we endured the relationship way past its expiration date because we weren't honest with ourselves and each other.

I can change another person if they love me or I love them enough.
While people *can* and *do* change, you cannot make them change. You wouldn't want them to change *for* you as it won't last if not done for themselves. You can, however, influence how they treat you. If you think about it, you've seen in your own life how someone you know is one way with one person and another way with someone else. By letting go of control, changing your own attitude and raising your vibration, you will have a much better chance of bringing out the best in your partner(s). Focus-

ing more on their positive traits, and feeling/expressing gratitude about them, is much more effective than criticizing. When you've been criticized more than appreciated, you probably didn't feel inspired to be your best, right?

If this person brings non-negotiable qualities to the relationship, honor your boundary and speak your truth, or the resentment will become metastasized. That person then has a choice to make about whether they want to change those qualities or find someone else who can accept them.

It's normal to yell at my partner (or other relative/ friend) from time to time.

Some people grew up in households where the parents yelled a lot. They always made up and said the yelling was just a way of showing their passion and love. They may have even said that couples who don't aren't really in love. This is NOT the case. There are many relationships in which the people involved NEVER raise their voice or yell at each other. If yelling seems normal to you, this is because you grew up in an environment with it. Realize that not everyone had the same experience, so don't expect everyone else to be okay with it. Also, if you don't like it, it can be changed.

RELATIONSHIP DRAMA IS NORMAL.

Every couple has issues and disagreements, but drama is not normal or healthy. Many of us are so used to it we consider it normal; you can choose a different pattern. **The cornerstones of a healthy relationship are commitment, consideration and compromise.** The relationship drama patterns to avoid are:

- Playing games

- Unclear relationship status

- Partner constantly checking out other people.

- Lack of responsibility

- Jealousy

- Gossip

- Emotional unavailability

- Excessive neediness

- Anger issues

- Playing roles laid out in the unhealthy drama triangle (victim, rescuer, persecutor)

THERE IS ONLY "THE ONE."

Relationships are a fast track for your evolution rather than a pass or fail hunt for "the one." We can have multiple "soul mates"—friend or romantic—each serving a different purpose. Finding a soul mate who wants to spend their life with you is a wonderful thing, but it's only as healthy a relationship as you are. The more you are the soul mate you want to attract, the closer you will be to your dream relationship.

EVERYONE BASICALLY EXPERIENCES
LOVE THE SAME WAY.

This is false, and a big source of pain for many. You may have been hurt in the past by being with someone who experiences love in a different way than you do, and therefore you felt unloved. For example, I was with a partner for years who expressed love with quality time, and what I most needed was physical affection—not just sex but lots of casual or thoughtful touching throughout the day. This was something he didn't want to provide or receive, and I felt rejected.

We'll discuss this more a bit later, but we all give and receive love in different ways. Identifying these primary and secondary love "languages" is important to determining compatibility with a long-term partner. Ideally, you and a partner would share at least one. More on that soon!

Another key to consider, is that some people believe that manipulation and control is a way to express love. "I know what's best for them" is a common mantra for these people. This is often learned behavior, but it is not love. Know what's best for you!

THE RELATIONSHIPS I SAW GROWING UP DO NOT AFFECT MY RELATIONSHIPS TODAY.

Whether we like it or not, we are ALL subconsciously programmed by the relationships we had or observed in childhood. Our perceptions are also colored by media and cultural programming. However, as adults we *can* consciously become aware of beliefs that don't support our ideal relationship concept and shift them.

I EXPECT MEN/WOMEN/NON-BINARY IN RELATIONSHIPS TO BEHAVE A CERTAIN WAY.

Attachment to gender stereotypes hurts everyone. Sometimes people pick up certain expectations or stereotypes of how men, women or non-binary people should behave, and if their partner doesn't meet that expectation, they become angry, disappointed, disgusted or humiliated.

For example, if a man splits the bill on the first date rather than pays the whole bill, a person with a traditional point of view would say that was a red flag. This can trigger female worries that he's not a provider, or perhaps doesn't like her enough. If he pays the whole bill, then his date might fear he doesn't see her as an equal or expects something in return. If a woman asks a man out on a date, or makes the first sexual move, she may be seen as aggressive or promiscuous as that is not how a "lady" in traditional society behaves. If a man—traditionally seen as the provider—makes less than his wife and buys into the outdated viewpoint of what a strong man is, he might feel emasculated. A woman who buys into that viewpoint might feel less feminine, or feel he is less than a man. A woman who is happier working and providing and letting the man stay home with the kids might be seen by society as a terrible mother or overly ambitious because women "should" be the nurturers.

Traditionalists try to place "male" and "female" roles on homosexuals or non-binary couples, saying "he's the man" or "top" in the relationship, and the other is "the woman" or "bottom" in the relationship, when the truth is, it's not that simple. It gets even more confusing when you are on the spectrum of these gender identities and traditional people are disgusted by your lack of conforming to what they see as the natural order.

The moral of this story is that you will be happier if you let go of societal and cultural expectations of how gender roles should play out. The healthiest relationships assign roles according to whom is better at what, regardless of gender stereotypes.

If the woman is happy being the breadwinner, and the man is content staying home with the kids, then that is a partnership that works. It is something to be honored rather than judged.

If judgment is coming up for you now, be gentle with yourself and ask if this is your belief or something you've taken on from others. Use self-compassion to see if you've been a victim of this mindset or judged and hurt another. This is something you can forgive yourself for and learn from.

To reinforce a healthier relationship mindset, I invite you to officially write down which of the false beliefs you no longer wish to own—those that have held you back. Then write down the opposite of that belief—a more positive, constructive one that you can embrace moving forward. Remember, you don't want to reach for such a highly optimistic belief that you can't fully embrace it. You may need to keep reaching for more constructive thoughts that you can believe, and then keep reaching higher.

Now do the final exercise in this section, 2I: Embracing New Empowering Beliefs on the facing page.

Congratulations! You have done a *lot* of resistance release work. I am so proud of you for sticking to it and working through the discomfort to get to a better place.

Before jumping into the next section, I invite you to meditate on these new beliefs and how they raise your vibration, opening of new possibilities in your life.

The Soul Mate Coach

2I: EMBRACING NEW EMPOWERING BELIEFS

False Beliefs I have Released	True Beliefs I Now Embrace
Examples: ◆ I have a better chance of being killed by a terrorist than getting married because all the good ones are taken by my age. ◆ I can't find I want to be with who can love the real me.	Examples: ◆ There are plenty of quality, single people my age out there if I just put myself out there. ◆ I know there are several soul mates out there who would be the right fit for me.

Be the Hero or Heroine of Your Story

"No one is coming to rescue you from yourself; your inner demons, your lack of self-confidence, your dissatisfaction with yourself and life. Only self-love and good decisions will rescue you."

Jenni Young

ow that you've used your intuition to release resistance, it's time to clarify your new vision and take some inspired action.

CLARIFY YOUR VISION

Ready for some fun? This is where you get to create your vision of the ideal relationship and start attracting it by playing the hero/heroine of your own story. Getting clear on what your highest self wants and needs—and knowing you deserve it—and living that truth will make you more magnetic to that experience.

Ideal doesn't mean perfect. It just means it's the right fit for your healthiest self. Soul mates are not fantasy relationships where you never fight. In fact, soul mates can push your buttons like no other. However, the button pushing should inspire growth rather than retreat into shame. The story arc of a soul mate relationship will be full of joy, passion and conflict, but the mates evolve. There will be times where the pleasure of being together makes you think you could never live without them. There will be times you may question whether you can live with them. However, when you take a step back and look at the journey, a soul mate relationship reconnects you with who you are and helps you live in alignment with your purpose.

Ready to get more magnetic for this person? The next step is to use your intuition to clarify what you really need to be happy in a relationship. The negative patterns you identified were important lessons in becoming more aware of what you need---versus what is nice to have.

The last relationship in my negative pattern taught me what I really need to be happy and content with someone—lots of physical affection and vocal affirmations of love—the very things my ex couldn't give. I was starving for those things, and realized I needed to shift that so I could draw in someone who wanted to provide those things for me.

What are you starving for? What are you dying to give or provide someone that they are happy to receive? These are your needs. **Try Exercise 3A: What Are My Top Needs to Feel Balanced?** on the facing page.

FIVE LOVE LANGUAGES

A book that can shed great light on some of your needs is "The Five Love Languages" by Gary Chapman. In the book, he identifies several ways people need to give and receive love. According to Chapman, the top two ways each person needs most to receive and give love are important to finding a compatible mate. Most of us have a bit of all five, but two stand out over the others. The five ways are:

Physical Affection
This expression ranges from holding hands and a loving touch as you pass each other by, to hugging and of course, sexual touch.

Affirmations
These are statements of love, respect and admiration that let your partner know they are seen, heard, appreciated and loved.

Quality Time
This is time that goes beyond being in the same room. This is

The Soul Mate Coach

EXERCISE 3A: WHAT ARE MY TOP NEEDS TO FEEL BALANCED?

Please take an initial look at what you believe are your most important needs that must be met in order to feel balanced. We'll continue to explore this in additional exercises.

Emotional	Mental	Physical	Spiritual
Examples: – Security – Boundaries – Attention & Connection – Achievement – Meaning	Examples: An hour of reading time daily –Learning new skills or ideas –Engaging with at least one person daily.	Examples: – 8 Hours' Sleep – 6 Glasses of Water Daily – At least one hug daily.	Examples: – Prayer time –Meditation time –Volunteer time

time you are engaged with each other in conversation or an activity that allows you to connect.

Acts of Service

Some people feel more loved when their partner supports them with acts of service, such as fixing something, doing a household chore, getting up in the middle of the night to take care of the little one so you can sleep, etc.

A Gift Giving/Receiving

This expression involves feeling loved when someone gives you gifts. This is not materialism. The receiver thrives on the love, thoughtfulness, and effort behind the gift.

TOP 10 THRIVING RELATIONSHIP NEEDS

If you still need some inspiration about your needs, here is a favorite "top 10" list that I think nails important qualities in thriving partnerships. Here is a paraphrased list from Psychology Today magazine, written by Barton Goldsmith Ph.D. See what resonates for you!

1. Kind, honest communication
2. Willingness to work things out
3. Sense of humor/fun to distract from daily life stresses
4. Sharing life lessons
5. Emotional support/compliments
6. Intimacy (romance, sex, love connection)
7. Shared dreams or goals
8. Compassion (acceptance and forgiveness)
9. Sharing new experiences

10. Owning mistakes/taking responsibility

Once you've identified what your needs are, it's time to start looking deeper at what you absolutely don't want (negative patterns of the past) and what you do want (the opposite of that!). Once you have this clarified, you'll create a desire statement for the ideal relationship.

Please do Exercise 3B: What Am I Looking for in a Soul Mate Relationship? on the next page.

LOCK IN THE VISION

Once your desire statement feels complete, reinforce your declaration to the universe with a short visualization. The most effective time of day to do this is the 30 minutes before you get into or leave bed. Both times you're in that powerful state between sleep and full wakefulness when you are still in a dream-like state but conscious.

When you are ready, read the desire statement, close your eyes and connect to the feeling of joy as if this vision were already a reality. Sit with that feeling for as long as possible—at least two minutes. If your thoughts drift, just gently notice without judgment and refocus back on the feeling and the vision. Feel the gratitude that you have already been given this gift—that it is already on its way to you.

I encourage you, as you progress in your self-discovery and clarity, to continue using your intuition to refine your desire statement, so you can become more magnetic to what's best for you. Use that same intuition to feel when you are resisting your greatest good, using the processes mentioned earlier to release those.

The Soul Mate Coach

Exercise 3B: WHAT AM I LOOKING FOR IN A SOUL MATE RELATIONSHIP?

Top 5 Things I Don't Want in a Relationship (The opposite of thes Evidence it isn't true e will help clarify what you want)	1. 2. 3. 4. 5
Top 10 Things I MOST Want in a relationship (Circle the 5 you need MOST to be happy in relation-ship)	1. 2. 3. 4. 5. 6. 7. 8. 9 10.

Exercise 3B: continued

My Desire State- ment: (Put the 5 Most Needed Things from Above Here; Refine the words so they have the most vibration for you and are specific)	"I love knowing that/I've decided that I'm in the process of attracting all that I need to be, do and know to attract my ideal soul mate relationship, which is/features: 1. _____ 2. _____ 3. _____ 4. _____ 5. _____ The universe/My higher power is orchestrating all that needs to happen to bring me my ideal soul mate relationship as quickly as possible!" Example: "I love knowing that I'm attracting all I need to be, do and know to attract my ideal soul mate relationship, which is physically affectionate, expresses love verbally daily, financially responsible and prosperous ($200K+ a year), is a partnership with _(things I want)_. I love knowing the universe is bringing me this ideal soul mate relationship as soon as possible."

TAKE INSPIRED ACTION

Now that you've clarified your vision of the ideal soul mate re-lationship, it's time to take some inspired action.

But not in the way you might be thinking.

Before you start dating, it's really, important to start living your best life as a single. That means not putting off anything you want to do that you've been delaying until you have a part-ner.

Live your best life *now*, in whatever way you are not. I invite you to stop playing the supporting character role in your life and become the leading lady/man of your story. Own your role as the powerful hero/heroine. In other words—and this is big—be the soul mate you want to attract.

One of the most common statements I hear as a dating and relationship coach is some variation of, "When I meet my mate, I will _____."

Whatever is in that blank, you must begin doing it now. It's important to empower yourself as a single rather than wait until a relationship arrives. You will vibrate at a higher frequency, make better dating choices and attract people who match that higher frequency.

For example, if financial freedom is important to you, and you have been holding out for a partner who is more financially successful than you, then it's time to get empowered. When we are afraid we can't do it on our own, we are in a fearful state – a lack mentality if you will. What tends to happen is, while we know we want financial abundance, but we don't believe we can have it on our own, we will subconsciously attract what we believe rather than what we want. So, you may want a financially abundant partner, but you will likely attract one who is not. This partner might be financially dependent upon you. This is the universe's way of getting you to confront your fears and overcome them so you can have what you want.

All you need to do is take baby steps towards that goal, whether it be getting a financial advisor, enrolling in an investment course or reading a book on a wealthy mindset. Look at the higher goal of financial freedom. They key word is freedom, right? Explore ways you can express freedom in your life right now. You don't have to have it all figured out before a soul mate arrives, but it's important that you continue your journey rather than stop and wait.

Sometimes a client will resist this and say something like, "but my dream is to ___ with my partner."

Whether the blank is buying a house or starting a charity, if this is your narrative, gently ask yourself, "why do I need a partner to do this?" This is likely a sign that you are procrastinating because you don't believe you can do it on your own. Whatever the reason is, it's important you take a step towards that dream without a partner. Perhaps you can do research on loans for first-time buyers or start a savings account for a down payment. Or do research on what it takes to start a 501c3, or volunteer at a similar charity to learn more about it so you can decide if this really is what you want. You may discover in the research process that you have a new dream and you can start taking steps towards achieving that. That confidence and dedication to your dream will help you draw in a partner who can align with that vision, either in a supportive role or active partnership.

The key is you want to develop a nurturing, authentic relationship with yourself in order to attract a higher vibrational soul mate rather than a project relationship. A big part of creating this relationship with yourself is better understanding and honoring your boundaries.

OWN YOUR BOUNDARIES BEFORE
YOU MEET YOUR MATE

Let's dive a little deeper into what is a healthy boundary versus an unhealthy one. If it's about honoring your needs, desires and deal-breakers we're in the healthy zone as long as it is about self-love and doesn't violate someone else's boundaries. Someone with a healthy boundary setting says no when they need to so they can allow more yeses into their lives. If the boundaries you've set are driven by fear, insecurity, jealousy and the need to control, then the ego is in charge which won't create a healthy, balanced relationship.

Once you're in a relationship with your soul mate, you may find that your boundaries conflict with your partner's. Since boundaries are not negotiable, together you will need to explore ways you can manage and honor each other's boundaries. No couple is perfectly compatible, so you'll need to come up with rules of engagement. It's good to know what your boundaries are before you get into a relationship as it can be stressful if you try and figure it out during conflict.

Below is a handy chart I created for you to get clarity on and own your boundaries so you can keep your energy focused on being the hero/heroine of your story. This means looking at how your boundaries have been violated in the past, either through lack of awareness or poor self-esteem. Then you look at how that held you back and impacted others. From there, you can brainstorm healthier ways to set boundaries moving forward—in a balanced way that shows up as self-love rather than a stop sign or over-correction.

These are your negative relationship patterns, which you can change just by being aware of them. When we see the pattern, we can avoid it much easier moving forward.

EXERCISE 3C: SETTING HEALTHY BOUNDARIES
If setting healthy boundaries is a snap for you, great! If you

EXERCISE 3C – WHAT ARE HEALTHY BOUNDARIES FOR ME?

Ways People Have Violated My Boundaries in the Past	How Did I Handle It in the Past and How Did That Affect Me/Others	What's a Healthier Way I Can Handle it Moving Forward?

need a little work there, I've got the perfect worksheet for you. **Please do Exercise 3C: Setting Healthy Boundaries** on the previous page, then take a break and return here when you are ready.

BECOME THE SOUL MATE YOU REALLY, REALLY WANT TO ATTRACT

Another important way to be the hero/heroine of your own story is to take a look at your life, identify what you want to change, create a plan with realistic goals and deadlines and start taking action. You don't have to fix everything to attract the right person, but you do need to have a vision for what your best life looks like, so you attract a higher love that matches that vision. I've created a helpful exercise to make this easier to do.

EXERCISE 3D: WHEEL OF LIFE EXERCISE

To start figuring out what ways you might not be living your best life, so you can set some goals to shift that, **please do Exercise 3D: Wheel of Life Exercise on the next pages.**

Give yourself *at least* few hours to work on this multi-part exercise, which walks you through the process of figuring out what part of your life feel good, what needs improvement, and setting some topline goals and deadlines. It locks in this work by inviting you to create a vision/desire statement for living your best life. This is a similar format to the desire statement in the last exercise. If you need a few days to do the exercise, so you can take breaks to process, please do. Just give yourself a firm deadline for completing this exercise or you might be tempted to avoid taking action.

TEXT CONTINUED ON PAGE 114

EXERCISE 3D: WHEEL OF LIFE EXERCISE
STEP 1: Complete Your Wheel of Life

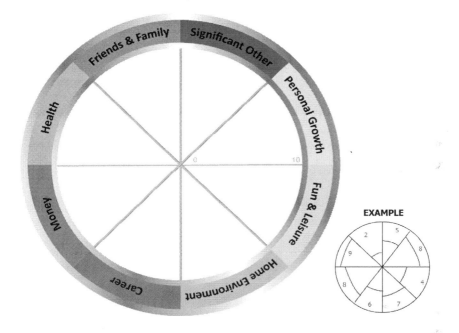

EXAMPLE

Review the 8 Wheel Categories - think briefly what a satisfying life might look like for you in each area BEFORE you attract your ideal soul mate(s). You want to begin creating that life to attract a more evolved soul mate.

Next, draw a line across each segment that represents your satisfaction score for each area.

◆ Imagine the center of the wheel is 0 and the outer edge is 10

◆ Choose a value between 1 (very dissatisfied) and 10 (fully satisfied)

◆ Now draw a line and write the score alongside (see example above)

IMPORTANT: Use the FIRST number (score) that pops into your head, not the number you think it should be!

WORKSHEET CONTINUED NEXT PAGE

STEP 2: Reflect on Your Wheel and Any Imbalances

Now, looking at the wheel here are some great questions to ask yourself as you look at each section of the wheel:

1. Imagine yourself a year from now with the same score. How would you feel?

2. How do you currently spend time in this area? How would you like to spend time in these areas?

3. What would make that a score of 10 and what would that look like?

4. Which of these categories would you most like to improve?

5. How could you make space for these changes in your life?

6. What help and support might you need from others to make changes and be more satisfied with your life?

7. What change do you want to make first? (rather than what you think you should make first?)

8. If there was one key action you could take that would begin to bring everything into balance, what would it be?

STEP 3: Take Action – Even if it's Just a Baby Step!

1. Based on your reflections in Step 2, identify one action for each area that you can take in the near future.

2. Rather than take the "all or nothing" approach to taking action, which sets most people up for failure, just pick 1 to 3 actions you can take over the next three months. You can revisit the wheel later in the quarter to identify new steps, if desired. Give yourself reasonable deadlines for achieving these steps.

3. If you are very busy or stressed, just identify the smallest step you can take now to get started and revisit the wheel at realistic intervals on your own or with a coach or mentor and identify new baby steps. The key is to move forward, with even the smallest baby steps. Your confidence and optimism will increase with each step.

4. Map out when you will take these actions on your calendar or task tracker to make sure you don't lose momentum.

STEP 4: Create Your Vision Statement

Now that you've identified initial—and realistic—steps forward, let's enhance your vision for the year to keep you motivated! Create a vision statement that states your intention and grounds you in the feeling of success. Create a Vision Statement and post it somewhere you will see it every day. You can add inspiring photos around it to support the vision.

"I am in the process of attracting all that I need to be, do, know and have, to create my ideal life. I love knowing that taking these inspired actions, and focusing more on my vision, are all I need to do. The universe will do the rest. Here's some space to draft your vision statement:

_____

_____

_____

_____

STEP 5: Fuel Your Vision

A key part of reinforcing your vision is to feel what your life will be like when you've achieved these steps and others you create along the way. Imagine the higher-vibrational soul mate you would attract if you were in the process of living your best life! An easy, yet effective way to do this is spend 2-5 minutes with your eyes closed—without interruptions--and imagining yourself achieving a balanced and satisfying life this year.

You can tap into the emotions you felt when certain areas of your life were satisfying, or simply visualize what it would feel like. If your thoughts drift, just gently turn your attention back to your vision and what it feels like as if it were already a reality. Sit with this feeling for a minimum of two minutes—longer if you can.

The ideal time to do this is the 30 minutes before going to sleep or the first 30 minutes after awakening. Revisit your vision each quarter and adjust as needed. Do not chastise yourself if you fall behind. Just keep taking steps forward and celebrating any progress. Meditate occasionally upon your vision and look at your vision statement/vision board to stay inspired!

As I tell clients:

A dream without inspired action is just a wish!

It's critical you map out actions to take towards this enhanced life path. They just need to be baby steps, but if you feel inspired to take leaps forward, go for it!

EXERCISE 3E: CHANNEL YOUR
EMPOWERED ALTER-EGO

Some of us still need a little help in living this clarified best life. For some, it's about a lack of confidence. For others, it's a fear of what others will say. For me, it was about the fear of being powerful; it was safer to keep myself small.

Whatever the reason you might be experiencing resistance to this best life you crave, I have an unconventional but effective way to address it—channeling your empowered alter-ego so you can fake it until you make it.

What does that mean? Firstly, let's clarify what an alter ego truly is.

Dictionary Definition:

Alter Ego = Person's secondary or alternative personality.

My Definition:

Alter Ego = Your authentic inner personality unleashed upon the world.

By my definition, the alter-ego is that authentic part of you inside that would come out if you weren't afraid. It's the part of you that is fully empowered and unafraid to be who they are. Beyoncé wasn't always the iconic diva you see today. In her early days, she channeled her alter-ego, Sasha Fierce, for courage.

Now she has fully integrated Sasha Fierce into her personality and is living her best life.

Because I was obese for much of my life, people tormented me daily, so I learned it was important to survive by being less visible. When I found my tribe in my mid-20s—a group of gay men in Miami who saw who I was inside—I was encouraged to let her out of hiding. Deep inside, I am a ham with a flamboyant personality, and the LGBTQ culture nourished that. I didn't realize it at the time, but I began channeling my inner drag queen, whom I call Mystique Royale. As RuPaul says, drag doesn't conceal who you are but reveals who you are. I began dressing in dramatic clothes, wearing wigs and unleashing my inner diva. By diva I don't mean I started acting like an entitled brat; I just began allowing my inner benevolent, campy queen to shine through. I stepped into my sovereignty.

At times people in my life were a bit uncomfortable by this transformation. That's why having a tribe who supports your authentic self is so important. Instead of my usual matronly clothes, I dressed sexier at work even though I had extra curves, which bothered some people. At the night clubs I didn't have to worry about the veneer of professional codes, so I began to dress in very sexy, dramatic costumes that some felt were a little too much. As a child I was accused of being a little too much, so when I got this shaming feedback, I armored myself with the love of my tribe.

My favorite memory from this period was when a couple of my gay men friends took me shopping for a bustier. I had this beautiful kimono I wanted to wear for my birthday party, which a dear friend who ran a nightclub was throwing for me. I wanted a bustier to wear under it for added interest and dimension. I had an ample bosom, which I no longer wanted to hide. They took me to a lingerie store, and I immediately went to the lacy ones. My friends looked puzzled but let me do my thing. As I tried on a lacy bustier, I hear them whispering. When I came out, they were lukewarm about the garment.

"Try this one on," they said, handing me an over-the-top, red-and-black leather one that would require a lot of nerve to wear. I resisted, saying it was "too much." They nodded as if to say, "yeah, so?" They insisted I try it. When I came out, they both gasped and said, "Wow!" I instinctively started to cover myself and they said, "Oh no, that was made for you."

My friend Scott said, "You're leather, not lace. Embrace it girl."

I quote RuPaul a lot because his message is so important and relevant now. He embraces body positivity and "letting people have it" with your fully unleashed personality rather than worrying about being "too much." You may find others you admire with a similar lesson about self-acceptance and confidence that you can draw upon.

For me, finding, channeling and nurturing my inner drag queen—decades before I even knew who RuPaul was—was key to becoming more authentic and magnetic to the people who would love the real me and support my best life. Today I tap into Mystique Royale when I approach public speaking, as she helps me embrace being visible and letting the world "have it." I set the stage for Mystique Royale with flamboyant clothes, a throne, and occasionally a wig if the mood strikes me—so I can draw courage from her.

If channeling an inner drag queen doesn't resonate, no worries. You may have a diva like Beyoncé's "Sasha Fierce" waiting to come out. Or you may have a superhero/superheroine inside you that needs to be rescued so they can save the world. If that doesn't work, perhaps you have a leading man or lady inside of you waiting to star in the movie of your life.

Let's find out!

Do Exercise 3E on the next page to help you come up with a strong alter-ego you can call upon when you need to. You may already have that alter-ego in mind but haven't allowed that personality to come through.

At first it may feel like you are playing a role, but I encourage you to stay with it. There's a lot of truth to the saying "fake it until you make it." Sometimes you have to play the role until you feel the truth of the character. If you keep at it, it becomes more natural and integrated with your personality—much like what happened with Beyoncé.

ASSIGNMENT 3F: WHO IS YOUR TRIBE?

My hope is that you currently have people in your life whom you would classify as your tribe—people who support and celebrate your authentic self, and are willing to call you on it when you forget who you are. In other words, they are your platonic soul mates.

When I started exploring my Celtic heritage, I learned a beautiful term for soul mate, Anam Cara, which literally translates to soul friend. My tribe consists of anyone who has acted as a soul friend in my life, whether they were in it briefly and followed a different path or stayed in my current circle. Throughout the

Exercise 3E: Channel Your Empowered Alter-Ego

Answer these Questions—without Editing—to See What Part of You Wants to Come Out!	
What qualities does my alter ego have that I MOST wish I did right now? (i.e. confidence, uniqueness, courage, etc.). Put at least one quality down.	
In what area of my life am I NOT showing up for myself that I wish my alter-ego would help me with?	
Is there a celebrity— alive or dead—that I most want my alter ego to emulate? This could be a politician, movie star, musician, scientist, drag queen, athlete, writer, artist, fictional character, etc. Describe them.	
Is there an archetype, zodiac sign, power ani- mal or superhero/super- heroine whose qualities I really admire? One I always resonated with deep down? Write about what comes to mind	

Describe your alter-ego as best you can right now (you can update it later but make it distinctive). What do they look like? What do they wear? How do they walk? How do they behave? Do they have mannerisms?	
As you review your answers, what are some names that come to mind for an alter-ego with these qualities? Look up names you like or translate words you like. You can also look up what names mean and pick one that resonates most. For example, my inner drag queen, Mystique Royale, got her last name by translating the word "regal" into French.	
What would be a mantra or call-to-action you can invoke when you want your alter-ego to take over? This could be a phrase that inspires you or touching an object you love.	

years I learned to allow the people who did not behave as my soul friends to drift away. This was not easy as I was often too wrapped up in not hurting anyone's feelings or being judged as a bitch. As I got older and wiser, I got more discriminating about whom I shared my heart energy with, and recognized it was not my job to rescue the lost people of the world. To be in my life now, there must be a give and take. There must be mutual nurturing and support of our success. I may feel compassion for anyone who is jealous, judgmental, manipulative or vampiric, but I don't need to fuel them with my energy. The more I spend my energy in productive relationships, the more I fill up my tanks, the more I have to give my mission in the world and the people I love.

If your tribe isn't your blood relatives, that's okay. Your soul friends can be your chosen family. If haven't found your tribe, don't worry. They could already be in your life but overlooked, or you maybe you haven't met them yet, but you can find them.

If you have some in your life, the goal is to make those relationships a higher priority if they aren't already. It's important to have people who will receive the same support from you. One-sided relationships are exhausting and are doomed to die an early death.

If you need help clarifying your tribe and making them a priority, use the 3F worksheet on the next pages to get you started.

TRIBAL MEMBERS YOU HAVEN'T MET
If you don't have any tribal members right now, or you would like to expand your tribal network, let's clarify who your ideal tribal members are. To do that, let's clarify a bit more about who

EXERCISE 3F: FIND AND EXPAND YOUR TRIBE

Current Tribal Members

◆ Who in your current life supports you no matter what and reminds you of who you are when you forget? How has their presence in your life impacted your growth? How have you impacted theirs?

◆ Are there people in your sphere who have potential to be part of your tribe but for whatever reason you have overlooked them? How might you find out if they're part of your tribe? Are you willing to take action?

◆ Are you giving and taking freely in the tribal relationships you do have? If not, how might you give/receive more?

Past Tribal Members

◆ If there is no one now, were there in the past? If so, what do you think are the reasons they are no longer in your life? Was it a natural diversion of paths or was it a relationship that wasn't nurtured by both parties? In hindsight, were there people who could have been members of your tribe, but you overlooked? Is this a relationship worth resurrecting or did it run its course?

◆ Have you invested in a lot of one-sided relationships where you give too much or don't receive? Or conversely, have you relied on other's support too much and didn't return it enough? How did that effect you both and the relationship as a whole?

WORKSHEET CONTINUED NEXT PAGE

Tribal Members You Haven't Met:

Journal about these two important topics for finding your tribe

Values?	What would you say are the most important values you hold that you need reflected in your tribal members? Write them out. A good clue is to look at the people you admire and note the quality you appreciate. These are also your qualities as you tend to notice the virtues you already possess inside, whether you acknowledge them or not. Some examples of values include integrity, courage, creativity, innovation, confidence, passion, playfulness, loyalty, optimism, humor, spirituality, tolerance, etc. Choose the top 5 most important qualities to you. These qualities should be present in your tribal members.
Interests?	What interests do you have that you would like to share with your tribe? This could be a hobby or cause you devote a lot of time to, or a shared personal growth or career goal.

you are, what you need, and what you have to offer.

Put Yourself Out There: Look for meetups and clubs for groups that share your interests and values. If you love hiking, and all your current friends are die-hard urbanites, you'd likely enjoy meeting people in a hiking club. If you are devoted to environmental causes, you can likely find meetups or organizations where you can find other advocates and volunteers. If you're looking to launch a business, and your friends and family are warning you about the pitfalls, it's time to join a group for entrepreneurs.

Not every group will have a vibe which matches yours. Don't let that discourage you. Just let what you don't like about one group clarify what you do want and hone your search. Before discarding a group, ask yourself honestly—and kindness—if it really is a mismatch or are you being judgmental and closed?

During one of your outings, take the initiative to ask someone you like to do an activity or have coffee. The key is to not put too much expectation on each outing or get-together. Just remain curious and allow it to be what it will be, detaching from the outcome. Eventually you will make connections that feel like you have come home. One thing to note is that it's also possible to find tribal members online—such as a virtual class or a social media group. My husband has several tribal members he has never met in person, but he chats with on social media. I met two of my tribal members in coaching school classes, which were held online because all the students were scattered all over the world. We chatted monthly in supportive pod groups online, and I came to rely on their wisdom and support, and they wanted to receive that from me. Eventually when I was in their cities,

I invited them out for coffee. Meeting in person only deepened these soul friendships.

Make a Commitment: It can be uncomfortable for anyone to reach out to strangers, but for introverts it poses an even bigger challenge. If you feel anxious about meeting new people, make—and commit to—a realistic goal for yourself on how many groups you will try in a month and how many people you will speak to before going home. When you find groups that most resonate for you, commit to going on a regular basis and don't let yourself off the hook because you're having a bad day. Remember the higher goal of investing your time and energy—finding members of your soul tribe who will energize and nurture your best life. That's worth a little discomfort isn't it? One thing you can do to stay motivated is create a vision board with inspiring images and quotes that reflect how you will feel once your soul tribe expands.

Trust Yourself and the Process

"Sometimes 'mistakes' lead you to
lessons learned and growth gained—all
of which help you to become more—
and get more—than you might have
become and gotten otherwise."

Karen Salmansohn

sn't this exciting? You're one step closer to becoming the soul mate you want to attract. Now it's important to start trusting yourself and the process.

Before you roll your eyes at me for the cliché, please bear with me. It's not about having blind faith and rushing into relationships. It's not about trying to be a saint and trusting people who betrayed you. It's not about having control over your future partner.

WHAT IS TRUST?

It's about being willing to be vulnerable and open, even if it scares us. It's about making a conscious decision to trust, with eyes wide open, giving the benefit of the doubt and setting healthy boundaries. It means focusing on all the ways giving your trust has produced the highest good, rather than the times you were burned. It means having the courage and confidence to trust yourself enough to give trust without the win/lose paradigm of needing others to earn your trust.

Wait, what? Everyone knows that trust must be earned. It would be stupid to just give trust, right?

Yes and no. You want to set healthy boundaries before deciding to give trust, but if you have the mindset of expecting people to "earn" your trust then you are doomed to fail. If you are coming from a place of fear and insecurity, then you will always have the need to be reassured that someone you love can be trusted. When they make a mistake, which everyone does, then they have failed, and earning your trust becomes an endless cycle of futility.

Here are a few different ways to look at trust:

◆ Doing everything in your power to get the outcome you want and then letting go.

◆ Opening your heart and believing in yourself and the universe's support of your highest good.

◆ Knowing that you are part of the process of creating and believing in your ability to attract what you want (even if it's with a little guidance).

◆ Choosing love over fear daily.

WHAT PREVENTS YOU FROM TRUSTING?

It all boils down to fear and the beliefs that drive that emotion.

◆ Belief that negative experiences in the past are doomed to repeat themselves.

◆ Belief you don't deserve or can't attract what we want.

◆ Belief that you are always bound to be disappointed so don't bother trying.

◆ Belief if you get too big or powerful, we will scare away love or get burned.

◆ Belief that relationships will hold you back.

◆ Belief that no one can accept you as you are—the good, the bad and the ugly.

As you continue to work on forgiveness, trust will become easier. Instead of focusing on what you are afraid of happening, shift back to what you want. When you catch yourself resisting attracting your mate because old negative beliefs or patterns return, and even feel a little needy because of it, ask yourself:

"How can I become more magnetic to my ideal soul mate right now?"

As you might suspect, the vibration generated is much higher and more magnetic when you empower yourself to create rather than fall into fear and needing something to happen. Now you can ask yourself:

"What can I do right now to increase my sense of well-being? What baby step can I take right now to be the ideal soul mate I want to attract?"

If you need inspiration, there are many guided meditations on the internet to help you get in touch with your higher power or highest self for guidance on what these steps might be. You may also choose to use guided meditations on my website *www.MySoulMateCoach.com* to connect with your highest self and even your ideal soul mate for clues.

CELEBRATING THE CLOSENESS OF THE MATCH

There's a crucial step in this process of shifting that I want to share with you, so you don't give up when things don't go exactly as you want as you start dating again. Abraham Hicks talks about an important process called "celebrating the closeness of the match."

This is an important concept to get because your inner saboteur will forget this concept in its misguided attempts to keep you safe from hurt. I see it over and over with clients.

What is increasingly likely to happen, if you are in the process of dating while doing the exercises in this book, is that you will gradually start noticing an improvement in potential candidates. You may feel excited, and perhaps feel like "this is it." Because of that, you put the book away and stop working on yourself. Or your expectations on dates might be unrealistic. As it's said in 12-step rooms, [unrealistic] expectations are pre-meditated resentments, either with another person or the universe. It's good to have a positive expectation that you'll get what you want in the end, but it's important to keep your day-to-day expectations realistic and not attach to the outcome of each dating experience. What often happens in this phase of transitioning upwards is that, when the new "close but not quite right" relationship blows up in your face, you fall into despair, tell yourself this whole process is BS and give up.

Don't do that.

If this happens to you, you need to celebrate the closeness of the match rather than give up. What you need to focus on is not that the relationship wasn't your ideal, but that you are getting closer to what you want. That means you are on the right track! This is when you should be going "all in" rather than putting a virtual stop sign on your forehead. If this is happening, it is a time to recognize it as a milestone of progress. This can help enhance the learning and raise your vibration, compressing the timeline between you and your ideal mate even more.

This is where you trust the process and that your ideal relationship is getting closer. This is the time to clarify a bit more about what you want. Use what you learned about what you don't and do want and review your desire statement created earlier.

Need a little help? Check out the next exercise!

EXERCISE 4A: HOW WAS MY LATEST
MATCH CLOSER TO MY IDEAL SOUL MATE?

Please use the helpful worksheet to reflect on ways your latest match was closer to your ideal soul mate and what ways they were not. It's important to do this so you can see that you are advancing in your quest. It also helps you see where you might need to adjust your approach.

EXERCISE 4B: UPDATE YOUR DESIRE
STATEMENT FOR THE IDEAL RELATIONSHIP

When you are done with 4A, immediately go on to 4B, creating an updated desire statement, inspired by Esther Hicks, that you can focus on and attract your ideal soul mate. Please fuel this vision with a visualization for several minutes, as you have done in previous exercises. I encourage you to post this updated desire statement in several places where you will see it daily, as a reminder to keep focusing on what you DO want rather than what you don't. This could be the fridge, bathroom mirror or office computer. Wherever. You can even post it several places. Make a new declaration to the universe with a meditation or whatever ritual makes you feel powerful and in the flow.

As you get closer to what you want, you may need to do this exercise again. This depends on where you are in your process and how much clarity you have on what you want and need. Please be kind and patient with yourself because you ARE making progress. If you can continue to trust the process and let go of the timing, it will speed things up in the end.

After that, please take a break.

4A: HOW WAS MY LATEST MATCH NOT CLOSER TO MY IDEAL SOUL MATE?

Example	
Values?	Competitive. Not ambitious.
Personality Traits?	Moody
Financial Goals?	Materialist. Doesn't save.
Spiritual Goals	Religious instead of spiritual
Physical Goals	Couch potato
Deal Breakers?	Smoker. Doesn't want kids.

Here is a clean copy for you to fill in	
Values?	
Personality Traits?	
Financial Goals?	.
Spiritual Goals	
Physical Goals	
Deal Breakers?	.

4A: HOW WAS MY LATEST MATCH CLOSER TO MY IDEAL SOUL MATE?

Example	
Values?	Contributes to causes.
Personality Traits?	Easygoing. Communicative.
Financial Goals?	Wants financial freedom.
Spiritual Goals	Wants to continue spiritual growth
Physical Goals	Eats pretty healthy.
Deal Breakers?	Compatible sense of humor.

Here is a clean copy for you to fill in	
Values?	
Personality Traits?	
Financial Goals?	
Spiritual Goals	
Physical Goals	
Deal Breakers?	

4A: HOW DO THESE LEARNINGS ABOVE CLARIFY FURTHER WHAT I DO WANT?

Example
I want a relationship with a person who:
◆ wants to make a meaningful impact on the world
◆ wants to make a meaningful impact on the world
◆ is active and a non-smoker
◆ is interested in and devoted to spiritual growth
◆ has a compatible sense of humor

Here is a clean copy for you to fill in
I want a relationship with a person who:

EXERCISE 4B: UPDATE YOUR DESIRE STATEMENT FOR THE IDEAL RELATIONSHIP

Example Desire Statement (Put the 5 Most Needed Things from 4A Here; Refine the words so they have the most vibration for you and are specific)	"I love knowing that/I've decided that I'm in the process of attracting all that I need to be, do and know to attract my ideal soul mate relationship, with a partner who: 1. wants to make a meaningful impact on the world 2. is easygoing and wants financial freedom so we can travel and do philanthropy 3. is active and a non-smoker 4. is interested in and devoted to spiritual growth 5. has a compatible sense of humor to mine I love knowing that the universe is orchestrating all that needs to happen to bring me my ideal soul mate relationship as quickly as possible!"

Below is a blank template for you to fill in and post on your wall!

My Desire Statement	"I love knowing that/I've decided that I'm in the process of attracting all that I need to be, do and know to attract my ideal soul mate relationship, which is/features": 1 _____ 2 _____ 3 _____ 4 _____ 5 _____ The universe/My higher power is orchestrating all that needs to happen to bring me my ideal soul mate relationship as quickly as possible!"

Use the table above to fill in what you learned from this process, so you can clarify and refine your ideal soul mate desire statement. Be as specific as you can without constricting your options. For example, it might be better to say, "compatible sense of humor" rather than "must have the same favorite comedian." Remember, you want compatibility rather than a twin. There's no growth or excitement if you're the same.

Okay, once this clarity exercise feels complete—for now—I recommend you update your desire statement to include any new must-have and nice-to-have learnings.

LEARNING TO ALLOW AND RECEIVE LOVE

It's time to talk about an important piece of trust, which is making the space to ALLOW these new changes to come in and integrate. This means replacing old patterns with new ones. It also means letting go of obsession, which just pushes away what you want. Instead, gently focus on your own evolution and what you want.

ALLOWING YOUR HIGHEST GOOD TO COME THROUGH

Once you have clarity about what you desire, you must make room for it in your life and allow it to come in. You absolutely must keep surrendering the need to control, which will always push what you want away. How many times can you recall seeing something you wanted within your reach, but you pursued or put expectations on it, and it went away?

This is the time to trust that you have done everything you can to get clear and remove resistance, and when obstacles arise you will know what to do. Allow yourself to keep trusting the process and let go of when and how your ideal relationship will arrive. Most of the people I know who've coupled with an ideal mate tell me their partner wasn't at all what they expected but they were a good match and had the most important qualities they needed.

An important part of this is to understand that most happily married couples have reported needing to compromise on at least one major desire in a relationship in order to stay together. I'm not talking about deal breakers, but it's key not to have the expectation that your ideal mate will be exactly as you want. In truth, no one is going to be 100 percent compatible with you and that is okay. Getting comfortable with that is part of allowing an imperfect person who is perfect for you to come into your life.

Then allow it to come. This means relaxing about it. Trusting that it's coming. Stop wondering about how it's coming or when. Allowing is the "knowing." If you know something is coming, you'll focus on something else, knowing that all is well. This is probably the most difficult concept to put into play. It is recommended that you put all these shifts into play in the less significant areas of your life first, or in one area at a time, and build from there (although focusing on them simultaneously can work as well). Focusing on less serious or lower stake issues typically yield quicker results so that you have the confidence to trust (allow) the process for bigger things.

The key is to keep it light and make it a game. Then sit back and watch what shows up.

HOW DO I KNOW I AM ALLOWING
RATHER THAN PUSHING?

As Abraham said, allowing means being ready to receive the abundance, love, well-being, or anything else you've been trying to attract. The art of allowing these things involves deliberately shifting your thoughts and feelings into the state of already having them. Your subconscious doesn't know the difference between your vision and physical reality.

One of the most important steps in trusting the process is to give the universe the space to bring your desire to you. If you declare what you want, and feel a sense of peace, you are in a state of allowing. In other words, you are letting go of the "how" and the "when" it arrives and are not obsessing about it.

If you find yourself obsessing about it, don't worry. You are in good company and can shift back into a more productive space. If you find yourself thinking a lot about "how" and "when," and are pushing for a result, then you are blocking what you want.

In Western culture, we are taught to fight for what we want and push for a result, and yet it's counterintuitive. Think about it. If you need a car and go to a dealership, you are already on the defensive before you even arrive, because you know you are going to get the pushy hard sell. This can put some customers into a state of anxiety—sometimes even in a fight or flight mode. You might see a car you like but hesitate to test drive it in fear the salesperson will have certain expectations. You might delay the test drive, or even leave for another dealership because subconsciously the situation doesn't feel right.

Savvy salespeople come in with the mindset of selling but allow it to happen—or not to happen—without pushing. They might approach you and just mention that they are there for any questions or to allow you to test drive a car—and then back away to give you space. You find yourself relaxing, not feeling rushed and enjoying the process of exploration. You have the freedom to really feel and see the car—perhaps even become emotionally attached. It feels good. You feel more trusting because the salesperson is confident enough in their product not to do the hard push. You might find yourself wanting to test drive several cars. This act of trusting speeds up the process because you're not resisting with defensiveness.

The same goes for attracting a mate. Most of us don't realize that we are defensive when we are dating. We are afraid we will get hurt or waste our time, so we put walls up. The other person senses it, and thinks you are "just not into them" and their energy drops. They might even take it personally and get defensive as well. Neither of you is being authentic because you are in a state of lack or fear of scaring the other person away.

If you find yourself doing this on a date, just gently notice it and don't chastise yourself. See it from a place of curiosity and just observe what is happening. Take a few deep breaths and come back to your body. See your energy drift from your head and into your heart. See the other person as another soul looking for an ideal mate. It may or may not be you, and it is okay. Ask some questions and actively listen. Let go of the need to know now and just allow the information to flow freely. Rather than see this as a high stakes meeting, see it as another learning experience. If nothing else, it will give you more clarity on what you do and do not want.

Simply put, you know you are allowing when you feel calm,

and you know you are pushing when you feel anxious or frightened.

If you start to get too focused on the result, it's a good time to return to shifting your attention back onto what gives you pleasure. Think about what you are grateful for and connect to that feeling that the universe does have your best interests at heart. This will quickly raise your vibration, which boosts your energy. Do something you are passionate about. Help someone who needs it. Do a random act of kindness. Take a walk in nature and observe the beauty around you. Treat yourself to something you've been putting off. All of this will quickly raise your vibration and make you more magnetic.

Test it out if you don't believe me yet. Or just do this as a fun experiment. Observe what happens when you're in a bad mood and you go out in public. Notice if people approach you or avoid you, as well as how they respond to you. What are you noticing? Then, at a time when you're able to shift to a more positive state of mind, go out again and notice what energy comes back to you. I'm confident you will quickly see a pattern. When you're in a negative space, people avoid eye contact or act defensively. They might even get annoyed with you and pick a fight. You notice more of the things you don't like, such as an ugly building, someone honking impatiently at another or mistreating someone. When you're putting out a higher vibration, people will want to be in that energy. They will give you a compliment, or maybe do something kind for you. When you go outside, your eyes will be drawn to what matches your vibration—perhaps a rainbow, or someone treating another with kindness.

If a part of you is cynically grumbling that this is an annoying

Pollyanna approach, just be kind to yourself and understand—from a place of curiosity—that this is just defensiveness and fear of disappointment. Remember that underneath it all, it's not a woo-woo concept. If someone is in a bad mood, aren't you eager to get out of that energy? And if someone enters a room with a radiant smile, don't you notice yourself smiling back, or feeling a spike in your energy?

Science backs this up. Like charges attract like charges. Opposites do not really attract. If you think about today's tribal culture, you can easily see that people do not form friendships or relationships with people who do not hold the same values, views and prejudices. They are attracted to their "tribe." I'm not saying it is right or wrong. It just is.

SURRENDER TO TRUST
One of the most effective ways to trust, is to practice the art of surrender.

Surrender is not failure, defeat or punishment. It is the point where you realize that all your efforts to control the outcome have done more harm than good.

If you have finally arrived at that place, then congratulations because that means the hardest part of trust has been achieved. If you are still a work in progress when it comes to releasing control, but you are still reading, then you are almost there.

Surrender happens when we understand that sometimes we don't have all the answers, and sometimes what we want isn't what's best or meant for us. My husband didn't arrive the way I imagined, nor did his life fit like a glove with my vision. But I knew that he was the person meant to take this journey with me now. It was a harder journey than I had wanted, and sometimes more than I thought I could bear; however, I trusted the higher part of me that said I was still in the right place with the right person, even if I didn't always know why. Of course, there were many times of joy, but I now I understand that it was the tough times that helped me confront and move past old wounds that remained hidden to me, and pushed me to understand unconditional love. That in turn has helped me evolve and step up to my destiny.

TURNING IT OVER & ASKING FOR HELP

Surrendering also doesn't mean that you remain in a state of waiting for something to happen. You must do the work, but trust means understanding you are not alone in your journey. Some unknown life or energy force is pulling you in the right direction, putting a series of learning experiences in your path so that you are sharpened and shaped like a diamond—if you allow it and flow with it rather than fight it. Another way to look at it is not to attach emotionally to the struggles, or it will trap you in that state.

The quickest way to know without a doubt that you are in a state of control or surrender is to get quiet and check in with your feelings. Your emotions are a sensitive barometer to what is really going on. The sensations in your body communicate information that bypasses the brain, which is a good thing. Our minds are important tools, but they can really trick us too. It can rationalize what's happening, or deny the truth, to avoid pain. But it is that avoidance that attaches us to the pain and keeps us from moving on.

So, if you want to know if your controlling ego is in charge, get quiet, close your eyes, and notice the sensations in your body. Are there parts that feel heavy or hurt? Are you feeling uneasy, unsettled or a sense of dread? If the answer is yes that means you are in a fearful state, which triggers the ego to try and keep you safe with controlling.

If instead you are feeling peaceful, light, curious or excitement, then at this moment you are in a state of loving surrender, trusting that what is meant to be will happen if we allow it to unfold without placing control on it.

CONTROL = FEAR

SURRENDER = LOVE

Another way to see the difference is to close your eyes and imagine you are in a canoe. See your soul mate in front of you. Where are they? Are they above you or below you? Do you have to paddle upstream to get to them, or do you need to put the oars down and let the river carry you to them?

We are taught that anything worth fighting for must be earned with struggle. Gyms chant the mantra "no pain no gain." It is true that pain can be used as a tool to learn and catapult you to a better place. However, struggling upstream is not the fastest way to get from Point A to Point B. Flowing downstream is. We are trained to believe that the path of least resistance is the "easy way out" but that is simply not the truth. Paddling upstream certainly can build character, but it means we are resistant to allowing the mystery to unfold, trusting that whatever we find downstream we will be able to deal with it and arrive at our destination faster.

Are you seeing it? In other words, "go with the flow" should replace "no pain no gain" as your mantra. The only creature that should be swimming upstream is the salmon!

If you are seeing it but saying, "Yeah Jeanne but that is easier said than done."

And I say, "Only if you allow that to be true."

If you change how you see it and make the decision every day to stop resisting and allow yourself to follow the flow of energy into the unknown, things will shift faster than you might imagine. As a Type A personality, every day I must remind myself to make the decision to release control. I am used to making things happen at work, but as I have let go of trying to arrange everything, I have found that the outcome is usually better.

Not only that, but Type A personalities tend to overwhelm themselves by trying to arrange everything—not just for themselves, but for others too. When we do it for others, we are telling ourselves we are being helpful, but we take away their learning and thus, their power. It is better to be the supporter than the arranger.

When you are overwhelmed you are not in a place of receiving anything—even if it's help. We become attached to that state of mind. One of the biggest energetic stop signs to attracting your ideal soul mates is to not make space for them. If you are often in an overwhelmed state, it's critical that you shift that pattern, or you may find yourself attracting potential mates who are not empowered and need you to do it for them, thus increasing your overwhelm. This is the universe's way of lovingly hammering you until you learn the lesson.

For the times you are overwhelmed with getting ready for the soul mate you want to attract, I have simple but effective exercises for you to do. They have done wonders for me.

The first thing to bear in mind is to resist saying the phrase "I am overwhelmed." That just reinforces your "I am overwhelmed" mindset that can paralyze you. In law of attraction, this vibration attracts more of the same, putting you back on the overwhelmed hamster wheel. Usually overwhelmed people are doing too much and need to prioritize what's most important and let go of the rest. One thing you can do to start is replace the phrase "I am overwhelmed" with something like, "It feels good to let go." You can also try these exercises:

EXERCISE 4C/4D: DELEGATING TO A HIGHER POWER
Now on to the next exercise, which is inspired by Esther Hicks in her law of attraction teachings. This will require you to call in your higher power to assist you, whatever that means to you. This could be the universe, guides, God, Goddess, Allah, Jehovah, Yahweh or whatever force is true for your beliefs.

Start Exercise 4C on the next page by getting out a pen and paper and draw a line down the middle of the paper. Leave the whole left side of the page to write down tasks, and the right side for ultimate outcomes you can delegate to your higher power. By ultimate outcomes, I mean the result you want to achieve by doing all the tasks you are overwhelmed by. By delegating it to a higher power, it means letting go of the "how" and the "when" of it happening and trusting the process.

When you are doing Exercise 4C about delegating to a Higher Power, I recommend not getting too specific about what your ideal soul mate looks like, as it can constrict your possibilities. An impression of their energetic presence is all that is needed.

EXERCISE 4C: DELEGATING TO A HIGHER POWER (EXAMPLE)

Step 1: Things I Want to Do Today

Write down everything taking up space in your brain that you believe you "should" be doing today.

Step 2: Things I CAN Reasonably Do Today

Take a deep breath and review this list with a more self-compassionate perspective. Instead of "shoulding" on yourself, write down what you could reasonably do today and still have time for self-care, whether it's a walk, journaling, a bath or playing. It's important to leave time for self-care, so you can fill up your tanks instead of running on empty. Studies show that people who have good-quality rest are way more effective—and happy—which makes you more magnetic.

Step 3: Things I Can Delegate to Friends, Family or Coworkers

Ask yourself if there was anything from Step 1 you could delegate to someone else? Sometimes we resist asking for help because we worry it will make us appear incompetent or we will be a burden. In truth, asking for help often empowers the person being asked. People generally want to help. If they can't, they may be able to do it later. If it really must be you, write down in your calendar what other day you could reasonably do these tasks and have time for self-care.

Step 4: Things I'll Delegate to My Higher Power

This is the most important step. Ask yourself what ultimate outcome you can delegate to the universe and write it down here.

Examples: Walking down the aisle with your ideal soul mate; – Traveling to Disneyworld with a soul mate and the children you have together. – Speaking at an event and seeing your soul mate in the audience or sensing them in the wings supporting you. – Sitting in a porch swing in your senior years with your soul mate. – Hiking with your soul mate in a place you love or always wanted to visit.

EXERCISE 4C: DELEGATING TO A HIGHER POWER

Step 1: Things I Want to Do Today

Step 2: Things I CAN Reasonably Do Today

Step 3: Things I Can Delegate to Friends, Family or Coworkers

Step 4: Things I'll Delegate to My Higher Power

After you have filled in the blank template for Exercise 4C, go on to Exercise 4D. Use this exercise any time you feel you are stressing about this process and exerting too much control.

EXERCISE 4D: VISUALIZE, VISUALIZE, VISUALIZE

Once you ask for help with the ultimate outcome, close your eyes and imagine a higher force saying, "I've got this," and allow this result to lift from your shoulders. Give yourself permission to trust that you are already in the process of receiving it. Engage all your senses to imagine the result already in your physical reality and feel your joy and gratitude. Say thank you to this higher force—and yourself—for guiding you through the steps you need to take and for bringing your dream to you.

Make a point of doing this visualization daily for a few days—ideally the 30 minutes before you leave bed in the morning or the 30 minutes before falling asleep. It's important there are no distractions while you do this. When you feel satisfied that your vision is locked in and that you are in energetic alignment with it, then let it go.

If you believe you need a bit more help locking this vision in, I recommend creating a vision board that you can put in a place where you see it daily. Gather images and inspirational quotes from magazines or online that reflect the future you want to have with your soul mate. I recommend also including pictures that reflect the future you want for yourself as an individual—YOU at your highest expression. It's also key that you include images about doing the actions to get there, such as online dating, seminars, going to meetups, etc. Studies show that vision boards don't work if you don't include taking positive action.

Put the images onto a board or create a digital board. If you'd like to give it a try, check out my free vision board video on *www.MySoulMateCoach.com*.

For example, two months before my husband arrived, I created a vision board with the following images:

Images with Soul Mate Moments
- ◆ Man and woman holding hands.

- ◆ Man and woman in silhouette swinging a child by the hands on the beach.

- ◆ Couple in silhouette getting married on the beach.

- ◆ Traveling with a soul mate in Europe.

- ◆ Couple exercising together.

- ◆ Personal chef cooking for a couple.

Images of Me at My Highest Expression
- ◆ Fit woman hiking in the mountains.

- ◆ Successful businesswoman speaking with clients.

- ◆ Woman in silhouette meditating on the beach.

- ◆ Me mentoring a younger person.

- ◆ Woman relaxing in a beautiful home by the sea with a dog.

- ◆ Woman spending time with good friends painting pottery.

Images of Me Doing the Work to Get There
A key reason why most vision boards don't work is the creator

forgets to include images that represent taking actions towards that positive future. For example, I included images of people chatting online, going on dates and relationship workshops. The reason for this is that studies show that vision boards without immediate action steps could actually demotivate you. When the brain sees your achieved goals, it believes they are already reality and relaxes.

I posted this for a while on my refrigerator and used it as a screensaver for my computer so I could see it every day.

The day when I figured out the last bit of the puzzle—branding myself more authentically online—I felt a shift deep inside that I could now let this go and let the universe take care of it. I took my vision boards down as I didn't feel like I needed them anymore.

You already know what happened the next day.

That was 10 years ago, and I completely forgot about that vision board. I was asked recently by my coaching professionals' group to do a presentation on creating a powerful vision board with clients. I realized I hadn't done one in ages and decided to make a new one with more bells and whistles.

Then I found the 10-year-old vision board and was astounded. Almost everything on that page had come true.

- ◆ I met my husband two months later, and he had a basset hound—the breed I had always wanted. He also had a young boy from a previous marriage whom I hit it off with.

- ◆ We got married on the beach two years later.

- ◆ I live in a home by the sea and my now elderly dog

sits underneath my feet.

◆ I'm coaching younger people—and older as well!

◆ I make time for creative pursuits—painting pottery and hosting a successful writers' group.

◆ I do a lot of guided meditations for clients and make time to meditate for my own clarity.

◆ I have a successful business without needing a partner.

◆ I lost 180 pounds and my husband lost 120 pounds.

◆ I make sure to spend time with my friends without my husband—even if it's a video chat.

◆ My husband and I travel a lot in and have a second home in Europe.

Although we don't exercise together, we did a weight loss program together and got more fit. We don't yet have a personal chef, but I know one day I will have that luxury!

So, there you have it. Once you have gotten this down, it's time to start putting careful thought into how you will show up in the world to show that you are ready to receive your ideal mate.

In the next section I will share important tips on how you can create a highly magnetic profile that will attract your ideal soul mate candidates. I will also share tips on how to date without losing heart energy and have fun!

When you are ready, move on to the next section and get ready to magnetize your mate!

Market Yourself to Show You Believe in the Product (You!)

"Authenticity is a collection of choices that we have to make every day. It's about the choice to show up and be real. The choice to be honest. The choice to let our true selves be seen."

Brene Brown

his is the step that most of my clients struggle with the most. Putting yourself out there can be scary, but it's important you do so in order to let people know you are ready.

Please forgive the word "marketing," as I know it can evoke cynical connotations. I obviously don't mean it in the traditional "barter" sense. The word is used here in the context or promoting yourself as a product that you believe in, so the customer who needs that product can know how to find it. You may feel like part of you needs to "fake it until you make it," and it's okay to feel that way a little bit because most of us are not used to promoting ourselves as a catch. We're taught that makes us look vain or egotistical, but I invite you to let that judgment go and look at it more as showing your inner light so the right matches can really see you.

Drawing on my marketing background, this means defining and promoting your authentic brand, so it stands out to the potential mates who resonate with that. In marketing, you always want to try and get your brand out into the public to the most people possible to secure as many potential "matches" as possible.

This means I highly recommend you do online dating—the smart way—and I can show you how to do that.

I can feel some of you out there resisting the idea of online dating. I have two questions for you:

1. How have the blind dates—set up by friends and coworkers who think they know you—worked out?

2. How many dates resulting from meeting in person have resulted in healthy long-term relationships?

Although all the negative things people say about online dating—such as catfishing (fake profile)—do occur, the truth is they also occur when you meet your dates in person. The newspapers are filled with stories about charming frauds who hunt for victims, approach them in a wildly romantic way, sweep them off their feet and scam them.

Of course, there are crooks out there, but if you use common sense you can easily navigate away from them. I've encountered them all and will share tips that will help you go from "annoyed" in dating to "enjoyed." The key is to not focus on the small majority of scammers and focus instead on the vast majority of real people who are looking for connection in various forms. At least one of them—probably several—are potentially ideal matches for you.

Many of the tips I will share do include information specifically for online dating, but many of them can translate to offline dating. Please stay with me and see what lands for you.

TOP 5 DON'TS FOR DATING ONLINE
1. Don't worry about the stigma of dating online.
The romantic "meet cute" moment in movies rarely happens because many of us are so focused on texting, posting, running errands and stressing about work to notice our immediate surroundings. I remember trying golf and watching football games at sports bars—two activities that I hate—to increase my odds of meeting men. Although there were a lot of men there, they were focused on the game and not in dating mode. When you date online, you at least know that most of the people are pre-qualified in that they are there specifically to date. And it exposes you

to many more potential mates than you could meet even if you were the most present-minded person in the world when out in public. For these reasons, dating online greatly increases your odds of finding your ideal matches. I would never have met my husband in my social circles.

2. Don't play it safe.
Be as authentic and frank as you can about your purpose in dating and what you are really looking for, so your tribe can see you. It's true that people on dating apps are focused on dating, but their agenda may be different from yours. Some may be fresh out of a breakup and are looking to get their groove back, while others are looking for companions to go out with—with or without sex. Still others are looking for long term relationships in various forms—including the kind where you put a ring on it! All are fine if we are honest about it, so we don't knowingly mislead anyone. Playing it safe usually leads to suffering because at the heart of it, we are afraid the dating pool is a puddle and fear scaring anyone away. That might work in the short-term, but it won't end well for either of you.

3. Don't post selfies.
I suspect that some of you, particularly those who prefer Instagram over Facebook, won't believe me on this, but trust me, do *not* use selfies. Even if you think you look hot. Studies show that both sexes find it a turn off, like people are trying too hard. Assuming that you are here to find a soul mate, you'll want to avoid deliberately sexy poses, as that will likely tell a soul mate you are not serious about a relationship. Whether it's fair or not,

this is how people universally see it, so why risk it?

Also, avoid pictures of yourself in a group, unless it's just one photo of you volunteering with an organization that is very important to you. But even then, you should be front and center with fellow volunteers in the background. There are several reasons group photos can be problematic:

◆ Potential dates might be confused about which one is you.

◆ They might not like the look of your friends and wonder if they will fit in.

◆ Someone else in the picture might steal the show.

◆ If it's a party picture, it might give the impression you are a party person not looking for anything serious.

◆ It can look like you're trying too hard. "Look how popular I am" is not a good look on anyone.

◆ Most of all, they want to see themselves in the picture with you.

4. Don't Obsess.

Once you've got your profile the way you want it, let it go. Resist the temptation to check it all day long like social media. The more you obsess over it and worry about when you will see results, the less likely it will happen. When we are obsessing, we are in a state of trying to control the process rather than trusting the process. It's truly best energetically to just check it once or twice per day maximum, or every couple of days, and focus on living your best life. I know this seems counterintuitive for some, but when we are focused on enjoying life, we project a higher vibration that will make you much more magnetic and receptive to allowing in an ideal soul mate. Worrying won't make it happen any faster, and in fact will often push it away from you. Think about how you've felt on a date with someone who seemed to need a relationship too much instead of projecting confidence. You wanted to run, right?

5. Don't Waste Your Energy on People Who Ask for Money or Can't Talk to You

Although most people online are just looking for an honest connection, online scammers are part of modern life, but if you take certain steps you can avoid them. Here are some tips on how to stay safe and enjoy dating online more.

Some scammers are crude and easy to spot. We've all shared ridiculous phishing emails where we have inherited a fortune but need to pay a fee to access it. The writing and grammar are awkward, and we delete and move on. However, many romance scammers are often psychologically trained on how to manipulate even the smartest of people. They know how to spot people who are vulnerable and take advantage.

However, what you have on your side are two secret weapons:

1. They can't talk to you on the phone or video chat, and they can't meet you.

*2. A sincere person will **never** ask for money, even for a charity.*

They will come up with clever reasons why they can't talk— such as being on active duty in the military. By the way, this is a common one. Be on high alert if the person contacting you on-line is wearing a military uniform. They may try to point you to a fake social media profile, which you can spot if you look carefully at the posts. The history will have a huge gap—as if they've hacked someone's account that hasn't been used—or it's just a series of recent inane posts without any real friend engagements.

There's often a "good" reason they need a little money or need to deliver you a package to hold for them. If it's money, it's usually a negligible amount they ask for after they've invested time in you, and you feel a false sense of security. Then they ask for more. If you are a highly empathic person, just understand that they are counting on your pity, and your caretaking instinct. Or they send a package that will surely involve an illegal product, or they just want your address for a robbery. Scary? Sure. But just rest comfortably in the knowledge that no one legitimately looking for a relationship—or who has healthy boundaries—would ask you to do something like this.

If you have fallen victim to scams in the past—whether it's romantic or otherwise—it's important to realize that you are in good company. It's important you forgive yourself and move on. I recommend in these cases to look at it from a spiritual level that someone needed the money more than you did, and see that good karma coming back to you tenfold. I say this because thinking of yourself as a victim will only attract more attention from people like this.

If someone you are sharing messages with online always has an excuse not to let you hear their voice or see their image talking in real time, rest assured they are likely scammers, married, commitment-phobic or trolling. If you receive a RED FLAG like this, it really is time to just move on without guilt or second-guessing yourself. Or getting freaked out about it. This is part of the shadow side of the world, which we need in order to appreciate the light. See it from a place of curiosity—a reminder that people tell you who they are right from the beginning, and this hide-and-seek behavior is not a quality that you need in your life.

As you become more experienced, you will be able to spot these people sooner. You'll trust your instincts more when you notice that someone's writing doesn't match the profile. They may be presenting themselves as a highly educated person, such as a doctor or lawyer from your country, but it is obvious from the writing they are not fluent in your language, have spelling or grammar errors that feel off, or use colloquialisms incorrectly.

TOP 5 "DO'S FOR ONLINE DATING

1. *Own Your Agenda and Ask the Tough Questions Early On*

One of the biggest reasons we suffer in dating is we are really afraid to be authentic about our agenda and to ask uncomfortable questions. We are afraid to scare anyone away. This is a good time to channel your alter-ego if you need to!

We've all been taught not to ask too many questions up front or we'll scare people off or simply spoil the magic and the romance. I suggest letting this concept go because most people waste too much energy on maintaining a façade of being "laid back." It's time to be more practical. Certainly, don't be so focused on your questions that you are interrogating the person, but at the same time you need to know if the most important needs are potentially there and the dealbreakers are not. One of the great things about online dating is, if you are up front about these "must haves" and "can't haves" in your profile, the people who aren't a match can bow out gracefully before they contact you for that first communication. They can do so without losing face or feeling that awkwardness that inevitably comes when they discover they aren't a match on the first date. A good idea is, just in case they didn't carefully read your profile, ask them online what they liked about your profile and if they have any concerns about anything. Offer to answer any questions they may have.

With this approach, I am inviting you to shift your mind-set and realize you WANT to scare off the wrong people BE-FORE you meet them, so you don't waste so much heart energy on pointless dates. You won't be putting yourself through the rollercoaster of excited anticipation to discouraging disappoint-ment. It's that rollercoaster that makes so many of us give up the game before we even really played.

I don't want that to happen to you. I also don't want you to make a second date with the wrong person because your hor-mones are saying "yes please!" I knew a woman who met a man online. They discovered there was a 10-year age difference—she 45 and he 35. They hadn't discussed any of their "must haves" and "can't haves," but when they met, they had amazing chem-istry and slept together right away.

This was a big problem that led to years of disastrous heart-break. You see, they had incompatible life goals and deal break-ers, and both kept hoping that their love was so strong that one of them would gladly give up their goals for the other. The thing is, even if one of them had been willing to do that, it would have been a recipe for resentment that would have eroded their love.

He wanted children, and she didn't. For seven years they played a tap dance around this issue, until one day he decided to sleep with someone younger who could—and did—provide that. He married that woman and started a family, and she found herself alone and heartbroken at 52. She went through a deep depression and swore she would never trust a man again.

I hope by now she has realized that it's not that all men are untrustworthy (or women for that matter) but that the hurt was caused by a complete lack of common sense in dating. If they had shared their goals and values up front over the phone before meeting, hormones wouldn't have taken over and caused such tragedy.

Speaking of hormones, that leads me to the next item on the "do" list.

2. If You've Just Got to Have Them, Run.

We've already seen what can happen when sexual chemistry leads us to lying about our agenda in dating and compromising what's best for us. Let's explore that a bit more so you can really understand the depth of societal brainwashing and its impact.

We've been trained to think we should have a big "spark" or "thrill" when we see a soul mate's photo or meet them online or in person. It's supposed to mean this connection was "meant to be" or the "ultimate sign" that this is "the one" and it makes for a wonderful "meet cute" fantasy.

That spark, we are told, is romantic serendipity, but is something you should run the hell away from. Really.

That excitement is the primitive part of your brain telling you this person would be good to make babies with. This is true even if you are past that age because that part of your brain doesn't rationalize. If you are feeling a strong sexual attraction, then you know that biology is in charge, not your mind or spirit. In fact, this drive can be so powerful we ignore the signals from our mind (common sense) and heart that you are putting yourself in danger.

If you feel that kind of "chemistry," you will likely twist yourself into a pretzel to be attractive to them and ignore all evidence that this person is not an ideal match for you. You will never feel relaxed enough, or honest enough, to be authentic with this person. Just like the aforementioned online dating couple, you would never be true to yourself because you mistakenly believe that the "spark" means it is meant to be. And you will feel anxiety when the other person inevitably pulls back when the incompatibility really shows. Or instead of anxiety, you may find yourself unconsciously "posing" to be alluring. If you find yourself posing with someone, you are not comfortable with this person.

Instead, see that spark as the igniter of a massive fire that will destroy everything you've built in your life. You would run from that destructive force, right? Perhaps that sounds a bit melodramatic, but if it helps you keep your common sense about dating, use it!

Your goal from this moment on is to seek out people who inspire a feel of ease and appreciation. Pay attention when people you may not feel intense attraction for make you feel "seen" as you really are and agree with your values and goals. The lack of butterflies—which are just fear of losing the person—is a correct sign that this person could potentially be an ideal match for you.

I don't mean to pay attention to people who repulse you. I just mean work from body cues that mean your intuition knows this person is good for you. If you feel like you want to sit closer, leaning in as you would with a kindred spirit, then that is the physical cue that is in alignment with your mind and heart.

I took this new approach with my husband, because the traditional approach clearly wasn't working for me. When we met, I did not feel a sexual pull, and both of us were a bit wary due to previous relationships. The conversation was not as easy as it had been on the phone, where we talked all night several times and shared similar values. I sensed his anxiety as well as my own, but I kept with it. The curious, observer part of me noticed that he had picked the perfect restaurant to meet—a haunted distillery restaurant from the Prohibition era perched on a cliff overlooking the Pacific. He invited me to the fire pit outside and got a blanket for us, and I felt a sense of déjà vu and peace. We both relaxed and started laughing about all these weird little things we had in common. He held my hand and it felt natural. I didn't feel like I had to pose or pretend. At the end of the date, he said he really enjoyed it but wanted to take things slow and start as friends. Since women often say things like that as code for not being interested, I was tempted to believe that. But my training had taught me that men usually say what they mean, so I chose to stay open and went to my favorite crafts class.

He quickly asked me out again, and soon the friendship blossomed into deep connection and passion. It led to times of great harmony and discord, and we both have undergone amazing transformations by being together, each embracing our life purpose and pursuing those with each other's support.

3. Post Current, Natural Pictures Doing Things You Enjoy

This is a delicious topic because it is probably the most stressful part of online dating, and I can put you at ease. It's not about posting the perfect, most attractive pictures. It's about posting pictures as you really are. Your alter-ego should be coming through in at least one of the photos! This will turn off some people, but the right people do not need a fabricated façade. They will be attracted to you, blemishes, wrinkles and all.

Okay there is one caveat though. YOU must feel good about yourself as you naturally are. You must radiate your unique beauty that comes from living a life that is fulfilling and in alignment with your vision. That energy will come across in photos to the right people—even if it's just a few. It only takes ONE right person to be successful in the dating process.

Instead of laboring over photos, look less for perfection and more for authenticity and happiness in your skin. Some of the biggest mistakes people make is to pose, Photoshop blemishes or post much younger or thinner photos.

Remember, I was 300 pounds with wrinkles. But my photos communicated my confidence. I felt sexy, powerful and interesting. I showed my potential matches these features through photos, comfortable in the knowledge that all I had to do is be myself, shining a beacon of light that would signal the right "ships" to my location.

That being said, here are some tips to help you further clarify what images to use.

Use a photo that is less than three years old and doing something you authentically love doing. Your joy and authenticity will shine through, making you more magnetic than any contrived photo. Studies show more people respond positively to photos when you are:

◆ Looking at the camera (without the "come hither" or "posey" look).

◆ Without a hat or sunglasses (which can make you look like you're concealing).

◆ Showing your full personality (a variety of close-ups and full body shots doing different things – at least five but no more than 12).

◆ Smiling with teeth showing (women) and smirking confidently without teeth (men).

◆ Participating in active outdoor shots (as long as it reflects your true lifestyle; if not I would include one resting outdoor shot with a natural location you enjoy in the background).

Bonus Tips:

◆ It's okay to include a professional headshot if your career is really important to you and you like the way you look in it. These days professional head-shots are more relaxed, so you look more natural.

◆ If you're not confident about the images you have for your profile, consider investing in an essence photographer. These are professional photographers who take the time to learn about you and what you want to convey about yourself. They know how to depict your special essence or spark—

including your inner alter-ego. It's a great way to boost your confidence if you have the budget.

4. Write a Magnetic Profile

If you don't consider yourself a writer, there's no need to stress about this part. You don't have to be a great writer to have a great profile. You just want to grab their attention and reveal enough about yourself so the right people will want to stop scrolling or swiping and read more.

Below are some tips, which I go into much more depth on in my "How to Magnetize " Your Soul Mate Online!" video on *www.MySoulMateCoach.com*.

What is the most boring thing about most profiles? They either say a couple of lines which reveal nothing and include a lot of overly sexual photos. Or they feature a long list of adjectives about the person and what they're looking for. We think these adjectives are specific, but they don't really say much about who you are and why you stand out.

Paint a Picture with Your Words

If you say you have a "great sense of humor" and are looking for someone who "makes you laugh," it doesn't help the reader. Humor is relative and means something different to everyone.

It's better to say something like, "My woman would fall off the couch laughing with me over The Three Stooges," or "My friends tell me I'm the Australian Jim Carrey," or "My dream date shares a bowl of kettle corn popcorn with me while watching John Oliver rant hilariously about current affairs." By being specific, it helps the reader see if you are a potential fit. Good humor is a universally desired trait, but one size does not fit all, and if you don't laugh at some of the same things it's hard to get through the times when you face challenges.

Fly Your Freak Flag

Invoke your alter-ego so you can be brave and authentic about who are you and what you're into. That way, only people who really resonate with that will respond. Those who don't like the full you unleashed can walk away before they even meet you and spare you unnecessary rejection. And you can avoid boring people who can't drink all of your fabulousness in.

I remember chatting with a man who ticked my "must have" boxes but in talking with him, he also ticked a dealbreaker I hadn't thought about before. Our profiles matched, but when we started to chat on the phone, he brought up something that was important to him.

"I don't want to offend you, but I need to ask you something important that I didn't feel comfortable broadcasting on my profile," he said.

I was wary, but also glad that whatever it was, it is good to bring it up now. "Sure," I said with an encouraging tone.

"Do you enjoy spanking men during sex?"

I kept my tone curious, without judgment. "Do you mean a playful slap on the butt when things get really good?"

"I mean a good, hard smack with a paddle. Hard enough to leave a mark but not enough to draw blood."

I was so awed by his bravery, and so appreciative that he honored this part of himself enough to put it out there. I told him that while I didn't think I would authentically enjoy that, I was grateful for his candor and authenticity. We both knew this wasn't a match, and we quickly wrapped up the conversation.

If you like to go to a lot of drag or burlesque shows, say so, and what you love about it. In my profile, I talked about how much I love watching "RuPaul's Drag Race." For me, this was not only because I wanted to attract people who might enjoy that as well, but also because it was important to me that I screen out people who were homophobic.

A conservative person might be turned off, and that's okay. I had one person write me a note about how Ru Paul was a "freak." I would now advise clients to just ignore comments like this, but I admit I got angry and felt the need to write back, "Yes, and I love his brand of weirdness. He encourages people to be themselves and puts a lot of love out into the world. Peace out."

I think it's better to just ignore people like this and move on, without getting hooked in like I did. The truth is you are not going to change someone's mind and you shouldn't waste any energy on people who don't see eye-to-eye with you.

If you love going to church and having someone in your life who supports that is important, then say so. Be sure to specify what that means, whether it's Unitarian, Baptist, Mosque or Satanic. If it's off the mainstream, it's even more important to be true to that vision and put it out there. Don't worry about the people who think that's "weird." If only a few people respond positively to you, focus on them and forget about the people who don't have the same values.

I just invite you to appreciate it when people are brave and authentic and resist the urge to judge and condemn when their views frighten you. It may be that yours frighten others, and that's okay. If we could all just allow others to be who they are without shaming them, it would be a lot more pleasant to date.

It's okay to be disappointed, but if we could remember to treat each other as we'd like to be treated, it would raise our vibrations and attract more respectful treatment. That would make the dating process more sustainable for all of us.

Write an Attention-Grabbing Opening

Even if you aren't clinically a person with Attention Deficit Disorder, we live in a hyper-connected society which makes most of us display some ADD-like behavior. There is so much competing for our attention that most people scan profiles like they do the news or social media—very quickly. You have just a few seconds to grab their attention and inspire them to read more.

The best way to do that is start with an interesting headline or line. It doesn't need to be particularly clever or witty, but it should really say something about you and make them take notice. This could be a funny quote a friend said about you, a playful twist on a common saying, or what your superpower is. There is no rule here except make it stand out, so it signals kindred spirits. Here are some fun examples I've run across or recommended over the years:

◆ "I'll Tell Everyone We Met at The Library."

◆ "Once You Go Jack You Never Go Back."

◆ "I'll Kill the Spider for You."

◆ "Looking for a Football Wife."

◆ "I Pay my Mortgage, Wear Socks that Match and Have all my Teeth."

◆ "Straight Guy with a Queer Eye."

◆ "I'll Bring Your Slippers If You Rub My Feet."

- "Ass-Kicking Nerd Who Likes His Mother."

- "I Don't Care What Car You Drive."

- "Sugar and Spice and Usually Nice."

- "Blond with Brains."

Follow the 80/20 Rule

Make the profile 80 percent about you, and 20 percent about your ideal mate. Talk about what you most value in life, surprising things about you, as well as talents and interests. Be clear about what you must have in a relationship and briefly what your top-line dealbreakers are. Be mindful of listing too many dealbreakers and keep the overall profile positive.

Some clients have said "But I don't want to settle!" Let's talk about that. In many cases, the people who believe that compromising on their wish list is settling simply have unrealistic expectations. Even in the best marriages, couples make at least one big compromise from their wish list in order to be together. The key is to really know the difference between "nice to haves" versus a true "must-have" you can't live without.

Too many dealbreakers on a profile become a big stop sign for candidates because it may appear you are impossible to please or unwilling to compromise. No one person will meet every "nice to have." In my coaching practice, I meet a lot of fabulous people who are alone because their expectations are unrealistic, which I believe is an unconscious way of staying alone and thus safe. I knew a coworker who posted a finger snapping, head wagging diatribe about what men would need to do and be to date her. It is no wonder she got no responses! It turned out that this was by her unconscious design because she had a lot of anger and forgiveness to work through.

Wrap it Up with a Conversation Starter

Sometimes people really love what they read about you, but they may be shy or unsure how to approach you. Make it easier for them by asking fun or interesting questions, or mildly flirty:

- "What's your guiltiest pleasure?"
- "How would your best friend describe you?"
- "What is something no one would guess about you?
- "What's a smart man/woman like me doing without your number?"
- "What movie character can you most relate to?"
- "What was your most recent Netflix binge?"
- "What do you most love about your work?"
- "What's your favorite thing about living here?"
- "You get an unexpected day off. What do you do?"
- "Milk chocolate or dark chocolate?"
- "Two truths and a lie... I'll see if I can tell which is which...Ready, set go!"
- "What's your secret superpower?"
- "Who's your alter-ego?"

I'd recommend not getting into heavy, beauty pageant questions like "If you could change the world, how would you?" Keep it fun and flirty.

5. Let It Go and Live Your Best Life

Once you have written your profile and posted it with love and pride, gently let it go and get on with the business of living your best life. Invoke your alter-ego when you need to until it naturally integrates with your everyday persona. The happier and more fulfilled you are on your own, the more magnetic you will be to people who want to support and share your world. In other words, be the soul mate you want to attract, and adopt the attitude that they will come when the time is right. In the meantime, you will pursue you dreams and goals rather than putting your life on hold.

EXERCISE 5A: WRITE YOUR PROFILE

Now it's time to get out a piece of paper and write the first draft of your profile. You can use the template on the next page if you wish. Once you feel like it's a good first draft, transfer it electronically to your computer, adding pictures to the document that you think would work well for the profile.

I invite you to choose at least one person you trust who loves you and supports your agenda to attract your ideal soul mate relationship. Ask them for constructive feedback on anything they feel is unauthentic and check within to see if that resonates.

CAVEAT RE: PROFILES

The profile template I provide is designed for online dating platforms which allow for larger profiles, such as *www.Match.com*. If you are using a platform with a very short profile, such as Bumble or Tinder, you might want to use the attention grabber line and conversation starter, and once connected you can send

The Soul Mate Coach

EXERCISE 5A: WRITE YOUR PROFILE

OPENER: Attention-Grabbing Opening Line or Headline plus Supporting Details if Needed. (Approximately 50 Words)

BODY COPY: Part One – Who You Are (80% of Body)

BODY COPY: Part Two – Who You're Looking For (20% of Body)

Conversation Starters

your longer profile. It's important they see your longer profile early in the process because it's a great screening tool.

ASSIGNMENT 5B: POST THAT PROFILE!

Once the profile feels complete for now—because you may find you need to refine it later, based on who you are attracting—just post it in your online dating profile. If you don't have an online profile yet, just pick at least one matching service that feels right. When I was dating, Match.com worked well for me, but there are many out there. I just invite you to use a paid service as that tends to weed out some of the less committed types. If you're unsure if a certain site is right for you, just try it and see. Be playful about it like you're shopping for something fun. Many sites offer a free trial, which is a great way to explore what interfaces might work for you.

Once you post it, I invite you to focus on your highest intention of attracting your ideal matches. Feel the excitement and gratitude of how this profile is sending your beautiful and radiant signal that will be picked up by the right people. Put it out there with pride that you're now at your most authentic and have done everything you can to attract the right person. Use your senses to imagine what it will feel like to have your mate with you—as if it was already a reality. Tap into that joy and thank your higher power for guiding you. Luxuriate in that vibration for at least two minutes to lock it in. Then let it go.

EXERCISE 5C: GO ON DATES

Preparing for Meeting—and Keeping—Your ideal Soul Mate(s)

If you have done all the exercises in the book and healed your major traumas enough that you are able to let a relationship in without repeating the same patterns, then I want to congratulate you! Getting ready for a soul mate relationship is not for the faint of heart, because it will stretch us and test us and help us step into our sovereignty.

Stepping up in this way, and reclaiming your power, can be scary for many reasons—from fear of failure and success to harming your friends and families. If this scares you a bit, it's a very common fear. But reclaiming your power by no means translates to taking power away from others. Empowering yourself simply empowers others because you are leading by example. Being your most powerful self will raise your frequency and attract soul mate relationships that resonate at a much higher vibration.

If you have bad days or setbacks, please remember that progress is not linear and don't beat yourself up about it. If needed, review the exercises in the book and reframe your thinking to focus on all the steps you've taken, and all the self-knowledge you've gained. Now that you are so much more self-aware, you simply can't go back to the place you were before. Whenever you face a perceived disappointment, reframe your thinking as we discussed, and see it as a lesson—further clarification of what you don't want so you can fine tune your vision of what you do want.

And do celebrate the closeness of the match each time you

meet a candidate who is closer to someone you can couple with long term. It's important to recognize these milestones, because they absolutely mean the timeline between you and finding your mate is shrinking. Staying open and brave will signal the universe that you are ready to receive and allow this relationship to come through.

Here are some more dating tips to help you go from "annoyed" to "enjoyed."

MORE DATING TIPS

So, you've posted a profile you can feel good about and you are getting ready to go on dates. Here are some additional tips on how to continue to stay safe and focused in your dating so it's more pleasurable.

Consider Buying a Prepaid Cell Phone or Getting a Google Number

Before you go on a first date, you want to talk on the phone first. I would consider getting an inexpensive prepaid cell phone from the store—or a Google number that points to your existing cell phone—so there's no way to trace your cell number. That way if the conversation goes south you can rest assured you can block their number and move on. As mentioned before, making a phone date is a way to help screen out scammers, who won't agree to chat in real time.

Consider Chatting on Video Before the Date

If the phone chat goes well, and you would feel better about doing a video chat before meeting the person, I would recommend creating a free and anonymous ID account on an app that is secure. If the other person is willing to do this, and engaged on the call, it's another sign this could be a person you feel comfortable setting up an in-person date with. Sometimes it helps to look into their eyes and read their body language to decide if this is someone you want to meet. Use the burner phone number if the app you are using requires a phone number. If needed, create a dating only anonymous email address and use that for the registration.

New apps are coming online all the time, and it's important to research which one fits your needs the most. Some of the popular, more secure video chatting apps include WhatsApp Messenger, Signal Private Messenger, Viber Messenger, Google Duo or Line. If you're not very tech savvy, ask a friend or a younger relative to help as the latest apps change. These apps offer end-to-end encryption, do not have video surveillance capability and the company cannot see your messages. They also have good records around data transparency right now.

Although Zoom got some negative publicity during the pandemic for security issues resulting from an unexpected surge in usage, the company addressed the issues. It remains popular with therapists, who must safeguard client privacy. I strongly recommend doing your own research on the best platform for you and trying them out, as new ones pop up all the time, and older ones poop out in the blink of an eye.

I don't advise using apps like Facetime and Messenger early in the dating process. You need to be friends with them on those platforms, which I wouldn't recommend until you feel very comfortable with this person.

I would only graduate to video if you feel at ease from your phone call(s). If you have any reason at all not to feel at ease, trust that intuition and move on to someone else. If you do feel at ease, keep the conversation brief (15 minutes) and end the conversation if the person starts to engage in sexual banter. I say this because there is always the possibility the person on the end could record your chat, so you just want to keep the chat focused on your goals. The goal of this chat is to provide a comfort level for you (and them) that the communications feel positive and comfortable enough to meet. It's a great way, if you are really busy with work, to do a first date dry run before investing the energy of meeting in person. If you do the video date and you feel uncomfortable, then you can block that person from calling your "burner" phone or block them with your video app.

Stay Curious

Rather than go into each date nervous that this might be disappointing, maintain an attitude of open curiosity and compassion for both of you. Notice the type of person you are drawing in, and whether you need to make any tweaks to your profile to clarify your vision further. Your date will be nervous as well but if you can stay in that space they will not be as likely to feel defensive.

Of course, in the unlikely event that the person is aggressive or abusive, then you've learned what you need to know, and simply need to say that the date is over and leave. Occasionally you will get someone who says all the right things during the initial pre-meeting contact, but when you ask any additional questions, they appear defensive. That is why I like to get across the must-haves and deal-breakers out of the way before you meet. It makes it easier for you to have fun and just enjoy their company. If you have covered all those important things but you are getting the vibe that the person is defensive, do a quick check-in with yourself. Ask yourself if you are in a calm place of curiosity or if you are feeling anxious and projecting more of an interrogation or mistrustful energy. Sometimes when we are afraid, we can project that onto someone else.

If you are coming from a place of curiosity and they're still bothered by it, then it's a red flag to pay attention to. People tell you who they are with their behavior right at the beginning, so don't overlook it because you are afraid to scare them off.

Stay Safe
Some of these tips might seem like overkill, and are not meant to alarm you, but I'd rather you erred on the side of caution.

Meet Briefly During the Day or Right After Work
The best first dates are of course in public and by nature are brief and take place during the day. I would recommend arranging a quick coffee or tea at a café rather than lunch or dinner because if it's not going well it's not as drawn out.
Limit Alcohol An after-work cocktail or glass of wine could also work if you frame it as "one drink." This could be a good option if you both are into wine and it can be a basis of conversation. Limiting it to one obviously reduces the likelihood of impairing judgment. However, if you are very sensitive to alcohol, I would avoid it altogether. I know that having a drink can make you feel more relaxed but use your best judgment.

If the person asks you out for a drink and you don't drink alcohol, it gives you the opportunity to say, "I don't drink alcohol, but I'll have a soft drink" and see how they react. Someone who is a heavy social drinker—or has a drinking problem—will probably be scared off by that, which is good to know now.

A note about meeting in any kind of bar, whether it's someone you meet online or offline; I suggest you pick the establishment because it is a good idea to pick a place where they use code words when you're having trouble with a date. I would ask friends or search online for places in your area that do this. Or you could get there early and simply talk to the manager or bartender in advance.

For example, in some bars, if you believe a date is dangerous, you can order a drink with a coded name that doesn't set off the date but alerts the bartender to call the police or have someone escort you to your car or a cab. A common one is an "Angel Shot" but most predators would likely know that by now.

Avoid Taking Your Car

No matter where you are meeting, you might consider arriving at the date in an Uber or Lyft or have a friend drop you off and pick you up. I would avoid taking your own car to avoid being followed to your car and having them trace your plates.

Remember, Look for Comfort, Not Butterflies

Remember, you must retrain your brain to look for comfort rather than butterflies. As we've discussed before, strong sexual chemistry can cloud your judgment.

If you're still not sure about that, consider a time when you went out with someone who you really had to have, and you slept with them right away—if applicable. The oxytocin often makes you want to bond with them, and you try and turn it into a relationship. But when you try, either the conversation doesn't flow or you're not in alignment regarding values and goals.

Look for the person who seems engaged and is curious to know all about you. Be more focused on the ones who you feel like you can really be yourself with—and are attracted to you as you are now.

Don't Make Assumptions

If there's something someone says that could be interpreted two ways, it's better to ask than assume. As they say, assuming can make an "ass" out of "u" and "me." Simply cock your head, smile and in a light tone ask, "I'm curious. What do you mean?" Give them time to explain. If the explanation satisfies you, but you aren't sure, be willing to give them the benefit of the doubt and keep exploring until you feel sure this is someone you want to continue seeing.

Be Respectful

If you really want to attract respectful, kind people, then it's important you look at your behavior and treat others with kindness. Instead of passing around "joke" memes that perpetuate negative stereotypes about relationships and genders, hit the delete button. If it objectifies others, hit the delete button and don't pass it on. It's not about being the "PC Police" but behaving in a kinder, gentler way so karma brings that back to you. These kinds of stereotypes and dehumanizing posts can reinforce old belief systems that no longer serve you in your quest to meet a quality mate.

If you're unsure, ask yourself if you would be a little hurt or offended if your soul mate passed this type of meme on to their friends.

Celebrate the Closeness of the Match

As mentioned earlier, if you start to date someone who is a noticeable improvement over previous candidates, but it doesn't work out, this is good news. This means you are on the right track and keep doing what you are doing. Instead of looking upon it as a failure and a reason to quit, recognize that it is working and moving in the right direction. Stopping now would be the biggest disservice to yourself.

Lay Down the Sword

This piece of advice is for heterosexual daters. Relationship guru Allison Armstrong has excellent data and workshops on better understanding men and women. Sometimes, because we have been hurt, or buy into societal assumptions about the opposite sex, we wind up creating the dysfunctional, adversarial relationships that block us from the love we want before it can begin. For example, she shares details about how women are trained to believe negative beliefs about men that are really myths that keep us from attracting the love we want and need. They wind up emasculating men and pushing them away when they are most needing their love and support. They believe all men are "selfish," "unromantic" and "players" when the truth is men really want to please their woman, can be wildly romantic and devoted. Unfortunately, if women are not willing to let these beliefs go and learn to communicate in a way that men understand what they want and why, they quickly turn "princes" into "frogs."

Another great teacher in this area is relationship expert Regena Thomashauer—a.k.a. Mama Gena, who shows women how to empower themselves and get their needs better met in relationships by clarifying their perceptions of men and putting more emphasis on pleasure. She says that women who learn how to make more time for pleasure radiate with a happiness that inspires men to come closer. She also suggests women become more aware of the anger they may be projecting onto men in their daily lives.

Being a "bitch" is a common rallying call of empowerment among women today and it's an unfortunate one. Be empowered, but if you find yourself being shrill, shrewish, entitled or blaming the other for your unhappiness, it's time to take a step back and have some accountability. It's time to retreat and give yourself more self-care so you don't feel so empty, drained and disappointed. Many women are unaware they are doing this, but if your partner gives you feedback that you are angry much of the time, ask them to find a funny, gentle way of letting you know, such as, "I'd be happy to do that for you if you sprinkle a little sugar on it."

Men are often hurt and confused by women's unhappiness because they don't understand how a woman communicates and thinks. Men can sometimes make mistakes in communication—without realizing it—that can give women the impression that they are more "into them" than they really are. They do what

Armstrong calls "trying a woman on out loud," saying things on an early date like "My Mom would really like you." When he says that, it means he is picturing his mother liking you as a person, but he by no means intends to have you meet her anytime soon. He may say, "Do you like skiing? Maybe we could go skiing sometime." He is just thinking of the possibilities but is not talking any plans—yet.

Armstrong advises them to keep these types of thoughts to themselves until they are ready to plan and act—such as meeting his mother or taking the ski trip. She advises women not to take these comments too seriously until he is planning with you to do these things.

In most cases, both people in the relationship are creating disharmony due to lack of understanding or unwillingness to let their defenses down.

Surround Yourself with Role Models
I would start minimizing time with people in your life who are bitter about dating and look for role models – people with experience in healthy relationships. If you're only surrounded by people who don't have a lot of success in dating, consider the possibility they may be blocking you from success by reinforcing negative beliefs or feelings. When you're in a relationship and having challenges, be mindful of sharing those details with family and friends as they can often be so protective—and non-objective—that they can give bad advice and hold a grudge against your partner. Occasionally a single friend may resent your partner for "taking you from them" or they may subconsciously want your relationship to fail because it makes them feel better

about their own lack of success.

It's better to share those issues with your therapist or a couple's counselor who can give you more nuanced, professional guidance.

If you really need to talk to a friend or family member, I recommend choosing someone who is supportive of you being in a relationship and has a good track record of relationship success. Pick someone who can gently point out where you could handle things better and not just reinforce your perspective—someone who is neutral enough to maintain an open attitude about your partner. The exception of this of course is if verbal or physical abuse is involved. Get the support you need from family, friends and counselors to get out of the relationship and move on.

Choose Happiness Over Righteousness

One of the biggest kisses of death in a relationship is when one or both of you are attached to being right instead of choosing happiness. In the pursuit of being "right," it makes the other person "wrong" and no one wins. When you are finding yourself overly critical and giving "I deserve" speeches, you are on a dangerous path. A new match will sense this and shy away.

Date Several People at Once

Once you make your shift, you will likely find yourself attracting several people, and I encourage you to try dating all of them until things become serious with one. Putting all your eggs in one basket puts too much pressure on both of you, and dating multiple people keeps your spirits up and gives you a better perspective of your options. When you date more, you naturally give off a vibe that you are not "needy" of a certain outcome, which makes you more magnetic.

Practice Gratitude

When dating, it's important to acknowledge when things are going well and let the other person know that you appreciate what they are doing for you. Let them know how it makes you feel. Appreciating the positive will improve a relationship much more effectively than constantly pointing out the shortcomings. Be mindful of sharing constructive criticism and choose your battles wisely. No one wants to be on the receiving end of criticism every day. That makes the other person feel unsafe and not very motivated to please you. Gratitude makes the other person feel safe and more generous with their time and effort.

For behaviors that bother you a lot, it's important to pick one at a time to deal with, so your partner isn't overwhelmed or feel like they are lacking. When you address it, focus on your appreciation for what they are doing right and give a specific action they can take or problem to solve. When they agree to take on the new action, express your gratitude and how much it would mean to you. This gives the other person a specific path to pleasing you and score credit with you—in a way that doesn't diminish them.

For example, if your partner brings you flowers, and you're love language isn't gifts but rather acts of service, then you can say, "Wow these flowers are so beautiful, and I appreciate that you thought of me when you saw them. I'm going to put them in a vase in my office so I can look at it all day. Do you know what I would love even more than flowers and would make me feel in-

credibly supported? Would you take care of dinners this week?"
Who wouldn't want to do more after that approach? When they
agree, you thank them and share how much it means to you.

Have Fun and Flirt!

By getting the tougher questions out of the way before the date,
it frees you up to relax and be your most playful, fun self with a
potential friend. I know your ultimate goal is to have a romantic
relationship, but establishing friendship first is a good approach.
If it's the right person, the rest will fall into place fairly fast.

Mama Gena talks about how flirting is a woman's birthright,
putting men at ease and signaling that you are receptive. When a
woman flirts, she is feeling confident and playful, giving her full
attention, which makes her magnetic. This puts the other person
at ease—and invites them to flirt back.

Sometimes women are afraid to flirt and be magnetic because
they are afraid it might make them feel obligated to accept a
date, when they were just being playful and exploring. Or if
the other person gets turned on and wants to sleep together, she
worries it might be her fault.

Mama Gena invites women to forget about using their
personal charms for partners, and instead focus on their own
pleasure and entertainment. Being flirty and having fun makes
women their most magnetic. It also takes the pressure off their
partners, because they don't have the burden of trying to make
that person happy. They just are. In several of Mama Gena's
books she gives tips on how to cultivate your natural flirty state
and practice.

Wrapping it All Up!

"Imagine your mind like a garden and your thoughts are the seeds. You get to choose what seeds you plant in it. You can plant seeds of positivity, love and abundance. Or you can plant seeds of negativity, fear and lack. You can also spend time trying to take care of someone else's garden. Or you can work on making yours beautiful and attract other beautiful people to your garden."

Jake Woodard

Now that you've taken all the steps to attract the right people, my best piece of advice is that—from now on until your ideal soul mate arrives—is to make time for pleasure and fun. As covered in the "Be the Hero/Heroine of Your Story" section, make sure you are making the most of the "between" time, doing things every day that make you feel happy and turned on to life. Some ideas include:

◆ Pursue your dream career.

◆ Make time for hobbies.

◆ Take yourself on dates.

◆ Make friend dates.

◆ Do exercise that you enjoy (hiking in nature, dancing, etc.).

◆ Treat yourself to spa treatments.

◆ Indulge in sensual pleasure (aromatherapy, silky sheets and lingerie, enjoying an artful meal, pleasuring the self, etc.).

◆ Buy clothes you feel sexy in.

◆ Get a makeover.

◆ Read a book just for pleasure.

◆ Play hooky.

◆ Do arts and crafts.

◆ Take a vacation.

◆ Plant a garden.

◆ Adopt a pet.

◆ Mentor someone.

◆ Volunteer / give back.

◆ Say yes to something you normally say no to – just to try it!

◆ Hire a cleaner.

◆ Redecorate.

MEDITATION – THE GREEN FLAME OF LOVE

And now, for a final meditation to reinforce everything you have learned and reset yourself to a higher vibration that will make you your most magnetic. You can do this exercise on your own by recording your own voice, or you can use the free video on the meditations page of my website, *www.MySoulMateCoach. com.*

Sit comfortably in a place you won't be interrupted. Take a few deep breaths, imagining with each breath in that you are taking in beautiful golden light from deep within Mother Earth. Imagine the light starting with your feet, soothing and relaxing, bathing all your cells with healing light. Imagine it clearing any darker energy and see yourself exhaling that negative energy so that your higher power can receive and transmute it, so it harms no one. Keep imagining the grounding, healing golden light from Mother Earth moving up through your calves, soothing and relaxing, breathing in positive energy, exhaling negative energy and releasing it to the care of your higher power. Keep repeating this process as it moves up your thighs, hips, belly, chest, throat, forehead and crown. Once complete, imagine the beautiful golden light breaking through the top of your head and see your higher power catching it, reflecting it back at you ten-fold so that it surrounds you in a lovely, safe cocoon of light.

When you are ready, imagine a pedestal in front of you. Standing on that pedestal is you—your future self—radiating at your highest vibration so that you appear as if surrounded by an orb of light. See, sense and feel your vibration and your radiance—both familiar and yet, different, because it is free of the blocks that held you back before.

See, sense and feel that connection between you, a ray of light joining you together—separated only by time and space. Feel the unconditional love and compassion of your higher self and allow it to wash over you. Feel your vibration rising to match your higher self's. Suddenly you see your higher self look to the left and hold out a hand, which is taken by your ideal soul mate. How this mate looks is irrelevant; what you are seeing is their radiating soul, happy to be with your future self. Suddenly your soul mate looks back at you over time and space. You see, sense and feel that connection, and the gratitude of finally meeting.

Ask your future self and soul mate what additional steps you need to take to compress the timeline between you, and then relax in the quiet and listen. Know that you will sense what you need to in this moment, and more may be revealed to you in the coming hours, days and weeks. Just allow and receive whatever impressions come to you now, trusting the information and the process.

When this moment feels complete, bow to your future self and soul mate, and thank them for connecting with you and sharing insights with you. Feel the gratitude and promise them you will follow your intuition and find your way to them. See them bow in acknowledgement, and suddenly you see them surrounded in a beautiful, soft green flame of light. Green is the color of manifestation. Send that flame energy fueling it until it grows and surrounds your future self and ideal soul mate. See the energy connecting you to that manifestation, owning the power coming from within you and fueling that flame of manifestation. Bask in the knowledge, that you have the knowledge and willingness to create this vision. Feel your vibration rising to meet theirs and fuel this green flame.

When that feels complete, see the green flame gently fade, and sense your future self and soul mate saying goodbye. As they disappear, trust that this connection is now established, and you can visit them in this place whenever you wish.

Now bring your attention slowly back to the cocoon, beginning to sense the room around you. Slowly allow the sensations to return to your body. Gently wiggle your toes, fingers and allow your eyelids to flutter open when you are ready.

Take a deep, relaxing breath and let it out, smiling in the knowledge that you have taken a huge leap forward in compressing the timeline between you and your ideal mate.

I can't wait for you to meet them!

PLEASE STAY IN TOUCH WITH
QUESTIONS, REVIEWS AND STORIES
Bringing soul mates together is my life's passion, so I deeply appreciate your respect for the work and intention that went into the book and am honored you decided to take this journey with me. If you feel you have benefited from the book, I would be

grateful if you would review the book or recommend it to a friend you think would be a fit for its content.

While I work on my next book— "You've Got Your Soul Mate…Now What?"—I'd love to hear feedback on how your soul mate magnetizing journey goes. I like to hear a good love story and am happy to offer support if you have questions. Please share any stories or questions on Facebook @*MySoulMateCoach*. There I'll share updates on trends, tips and activities and get feedback from readers on information they'd be interested in. You can also reach out to us for additional support at *www.MySoulMateCoach.com*.

Thank you for trusting me with your Soul Mate Attraction journey! I am confident that, if you've taken all these steps—including stepping into your sovereignty, living your best life and staying aware—you have significantly shortened the timeline between you and your ideal soul mate relationship. From there on it's a whole other adventure, which will be epic. I believe soul mates coming together is more important than ever, and I would love to hear what magic you are making together in the world!

Printed in Poland
by Amazon Fulfillment
Poland Sp. z o.o., Wrocław

65345122R00122